Conducting ONLINE Surveys

Conducting ONLINE Surveys

VALERIE M. SUE
California State University, East Bay

LOIS A. RITTER
California State University, East Bay

SAGE Publications
Los Angeles · London · New Delhi · Singapore

For information:

Sage Publications, Inc.
2455 Teller Road
Thousand Oaks, California 91320
E-mail: order@sagepub.com

Sage Publications India Pvt. Ltd.
B 1/I 1 Mohan Cooperative
 Industrial Area
Mathura Road, New Delhi
India 110 044

Sage Publications Ltd.
1 Oliver's Yard
55 City Road
London EC1Y 1SP
United Kingdom

Sage Publications Asia-Pacific
 Pte. Ltd.
33 Pekin Street #02-01
Far East Square
Singapore 048763

Printed in the United States of America

Library of Congress Cataloging-in-Publication Data

Sue, Valerie M.
Conducting online surveys/Valerie M. Sue and Lois A. Ritter.
    p. cm.
Includes bibliographical references and index.
ISBN-13: 978-1-4129-3753-5 (cloth: alk. paper)
ISBN-13: 978-1-4129-3754-2 (pbk.: alk. paper)
    1. Social surveys—Methodology. 2. Internet questionnaires.
I. Ritter, Lois A. II. Title.
HM538.S84 2007
301.028—dc22   2006029888

This book is printed on acid-free paper.

10   11   12   11   10   9   8   7   6   5   4   3   2

Acquiring Editor:	Lisa Cuevas Shaw
Editorial Assistant:	Karen Margrethe Greene
Production Editor:	Beth A. Bernstein
Typesetter:	C&M Digitals (P) Ltd.
Indexer:	Ellen Slavitz
Graphic Designer:	Edgar Ebarca
Marketing Manager:	Stephanie Adams

Contents

List of Tables & Figures

Preface

The pace of modern life and the rapid development of technology have had a significant impact on survey methodology. The increasing use of cell phones, fewer land phone lines, and do-not-call lists make traditional phone surveys increasingly difficult to administer. The abundance of sales appeals and other "junk" mail render postal mail surveys ineffective for many purposes. And for many researchers, the cost of face-to-face survey administration is prohibitive. Online surveys are a promising way to deal with many of these issues.

The proliferation of the World Wide Web and the diffusion of e-mail combined with an increase in the availability of software and Web hosts for developing and disseminating surveys have created many opportunities and challenges for survey researchers. These technological opportunities and problems necessitate up-to-date instruction in online survey research methodology.

Purpose

The primary purpose of this book is to address the needs of researchers who would like to use the Internet to conduct survey research. Some of the issues we cover, such as sampling from online populations, developing the online questionnaire, and administering the survey, are unique to Internet surveys. Others, such as creating reliable and valid survey questions, data analysis strategies, and writing the survey report, are common to all survey environments. While excellent book-length treatments of some of these topics exist elsewhere, it is our aim to provide a single resource that covers the particulars of online surveys as well as the basics of the survey research process.

Audience

This text will be valuable to individuals who intend to use online surveys for academic or professional pursuits. Although introductory courses in statistics or research methods are helpful, they are not necessary prerequisites to grasp the concepts presented herein. We have tried to ensure that the material is accessible to general audiences.

This book may be successfully used as a supplemental text in undergraduate research methods courses in business, science, and the social sciences; by graduate students working on theses or dissertations; and for self-study by professionals in marketing research, opinion polling, scientific consulting, and other areas of business and government.

Organization

The organization of this text follows the general progression of the research process. We begin with a broad discussion of survey research and compare online survey administration with telephone, postal mail, and face-to-face techniques. We also point out the situations for which online surveys are most effective. In Chapter 2, we examine the benefits and limitations of e-mail and Web-based surveys. We also present factors to consider when purchasing software and deciding on a Web survey host.

Chapter 3 covers sampling strategies appropriate to online surveys, and Chapter 4 discusses the guidelines for writing good survey questions. Chapters 5 and 6 offer suggestions for designing and conducting the survey, and Chapters 7 and 8 focus on data analysis and presentation.

As anyone who has ever conducted a research project knows, the process is seldom neat and linear. We have written these chapters so that readers may direct their attention to particular areas that meet their immediate needs. While a novice researcher may find it helpful to begin at Chapter 1 and progress chapter by chapter, an intermediate-level investigator might begin with Chapters 2 and 3 and then jump to Chapters 5 and 6 without loss of continuity.

Acknowledgments

Two names appear on the cover of this book; however, many individuals have contributed to its completion. We are grateful to the staff at Sage Publications, particularly Lisa Cuevas Shaw, Karen Greene, and Beth Bernstein, for their support and assistance in moving this project from idea to finished product. We are also thankful to the reviewers, who provided numerous thoughtful comments and helpful suggestions. Finally, we are indebted to our families for their encouragement and patience.

1

Introduction

L   ow-cost computing and the rapid growth of the Internet have created
    a new environment for conducting survey research. Like all research
methods, online survey research has benefits and drawbacks; the method
works well for some research projects but is by no means an appropriate
data collection tool for all projects. This book provides practical information
for researchers who are considering using the Internet to conduct surveys.
We will evaluate the advantages and disadvantages of using the Internet to
collect survey data and offer guidelines for the creation and implementation
of Internet surveys. The topics covered herein will be of interest to survey
researchers in a wide variety of academic and professional settings who wish
to evaluate their options for data collection and analysis.

In this chapter, we begin by reviewing some basic concepts about the survey process in general, discuss the conditions under which online surveys
may be appropriate, and present a review of the research surrounding online
survey research.

What Is a Survey?

A survey is a system for collecting information. Often in discussions about
conducting surveys, emphasis is incorrectly placed on questionnaires. To
employ surveys most effectively, it is important to understand that a questionnaire is one element of a process that begins with defining objectives and
ends with data analysis and reporting of results (Dillman, 2000). In explicat-
ing *total survey design* (TSD), Fowler (2002) emphasized that taking a view

of the entire survey process is critical to the success of a research project. TSD requires that researchers take a holistic approach by considering all aspects of the survey process. In doing so, one increases the likelihood of collecting data that adequately address the study's objectives while balancing time and cost constraints.

The basic steps in the survey process are the same for all types of surveys:

- Define objectives.
  - o Determine what you want to know and why.
  - o Think about who will look at the results.
  - o Consider the influence of external funding sources.

- Define the population and choose a **sampling frame.**
  - o Look for an existing sampling frame or create a sampling frame.
  - o Consider probability and nonprobability sampling strategies.

- Design a data collection strategy.
  - o Evaluate time and budget constraints.
  - o Estimate available resources.
  - o Choose a survey administration method.

- Develop a questionnaire.
  - o Write the questions.
  - o **Pretest** the questionnaire.

- Collect data.
  - o Monitor responses.
  - o Employ follow-ups as needed.

- Manage the data.
  - o Create a codebook.
  - o Input or export the data.
  - o Clean the data.
  - o Transform the data.

- Analyze the data.
- Disseminate the results; for example, write a report or give an oral presentation.
  - o Create visual aids for the dissemination process.

The traditional methods for administering surveys include telephone interviewing, self-administered mail questionnaires, and face-to-face interviewing. Added to these methods is a host of new techniques made available by the development of the Internet, most notably e-mail and Web-based surveys. In e-mail surveys, the questionnaire is either contained in the body of an e-mail message or included as an attachment. In most cases, the **respondent** can complete the questionnaire by replying to the original e-mail. In Web-based surveys, the questionnaire resides on a Web site. The respondent visits the site, either by clicking on a **hyperlink** in an e-mail message or by typing the Web address into a browser window, and completes the questionnaire.

As with any new tool, Internet surveys provide a wealth of opportunities and challenges for researchers. It is important that researchers recognize these opportunities and limitations so that they may make informed decisions when selecting a data collection method. It is doubtful that Internet-based surveys will replace traditional methods of data collection; rather, this method will likely take its place as an alternative, and perhaps complement, to existing techniques.

Why Is a Book Specific to Online Survey Research Needed?

Online survey research is still in its infancy. The method has been touted as the wave of the future, with supporters citing speedy response, low cost, and easy fielding as major benefits, while detractors lob harsh criticism about the low response rates and claims that **samples** do not adequately represent **populations**. Although the particulars of the technology are new, the controversy surrounding the research methodology is not. In fact, much of the current debate about online surveys is reminiscent of a previous era when mail and telephone surveys were met with suspicion. About 30 years ago, survey authority Don Dillman (1978) noted

> Neither mail nor telephone has been considered anything more than a poor substitute for the much heralded face-to-face interview. Perhaps this view is justified, because the two methods had many deficiencies and problems. Surveys by mail typically elicited extremely low response rates, even with short questionnaires . . . Further, it is not possible to reach many people with mail questionnaires; among those to whom questionnaires could be delivered, the best educated were far more likely to respond. Even completed questionnaires left much to be desired . . . It is not surprising, then, that users of the mail questionnaire treated response rates well below 50 percent as "acceptable" and explained away problems of data quality with disclaimers such as, "this is the best we can expect from a mail questionnaire." (pp. 1–2)

Substitute the word *online* in place of *mail* in the above quotation, and you would have a good indication of the contemporary discussion surrounding the use of online surveys. In the decades since Dillman wrote these words, there has been a plethora of methodological research that has resulted in techniques for mitigating the deficiencies inherent in the mail and telephone survey methods. It is likely that in the decades to come, researchers will develop procedures for similarly compensating for the limitations of online surveys.

As stated earlier, all surveys, whether conducted by mail, by telephone, or online, have common features. All require clear objectives, well-crafted questionnaires, a sampling strategy, and so on. However, the idiosyncrasies of online surveys with respect to planning, development, distribution, and analysis of the results warrant detailed attention.

Planning

When using an online survey, the sample is limited to those who have e-mail and/or Internet access. Therefore, researchers need to ensure that the target audience is being reached and that coverage bias does not exist. Confidentiality and anonymity issues also need to be addressed differently than when using a traditional method.

Development

Developing the online survey instrument offers opportunities for interactivity not previously available.

Distribution

Distribution of online surveys entails different strategies for identifying and reaching the **target population**. Also, traditional incentives such as coupons, free pens, stickers, and so on must be reevaluated when the survey is conducted online.

Analysis

Online surveys offer the opportunity for direct data entry, greatly reducing staff time, data entry errors, and expense. However, this convenience is coupled with limitations with respect to the number and type of questions that may be placed on the questionnaire.

When Should an Online Survey Be Used?

Online surveys are not appropriate for every research project. Below are some questions for researchers who are considering using an online survey for data collection:

1. *What is the desired sample size, and how is the sample distributed geographically?* If the sample size is fairly large and widely distributed geographically, online administration is a good option. Online surveys typically involve higher start-up costs than other methods but become cost-effective as the number of completed questionnaires increases. It is therefore inefficient to conduct an online survey when only a few respondents are required. Additionally, if the respondents are concentrated in a narrow geographic region, telephonic or face-to-face interviews are feasible, albeit more expensive, options, which may result in a higher response rate, thereby reducing nonresponse error.

2. *What are the time constraints?* Online surveys have the potential for fast turnaround. E-mail communication is instantaneous, whereas postal mail must be physically delivered, obviously taking more time. Researchers should be cautioned, however, about making the general conclusion that Internet surveys are always faster than other methods. It is important to consider the total time required to administer the survey; this may include an advance letter or e-mail message plus one or more follow-up reminders. Moreover, to achieve a sufficiently high response rate, a researcher may choose to keep an Internet survey in the field for an extended period of time.

3. *Does the questionnaire deal with sensitive information?* If so, anonymity might be a concern. Participants who are asked to respond to a questionnaire by replying to an e-mail will lose their anonymity. If, however, participants are directed to a Web site to complete the questionnaire, some measure of anonymity can be promised. With regard to socially desirable responses, online surveys are similar to self-administered postal mail questionnaires. Because there is no interviewer on the phone or in person, respondents tend to feel safer providing honest answers in an online environment.

4. *Who is your target?* Clearly, Internet surveys require that target respondents have access to the Internet. Physical, psychological, or financial limitations to computer technology may prohibit the use of online surveys for certain populations. Online surveys work best in closed populations where the potential respondents are known to have e-mail or Internet access—for example, a group of employees at a company, students at a university, or members of a professional association.

5. *Is there a sampling frame?* Responses to online surveys are greatest when respondents are first contacted by e-mail. If you do not have an e-mail list, can one be created or obtained? Government agencies, businesses, and educational institutions maintain e-mail lists of their constituencies. Access to the appropriate list makes an online survey a reasonable choice.

The alternative to using an organization's list would be to advertise the survey, perhaps on Web sites or in promotional literature, directing potential respondents to a Web site containing the questionnaire. Using this alternative deprives the researcher of the benefits of speed and efficiency that an existing list provides and introduces validity concerns related to respondent self-selection into the study.

6. *Is a convenience sample sufficient, or is a probability sample necessary?* To make inferences about underlying populations based on sample statistics, it is necessary to select a probability sample of respondents. Because there is no general population e-mail list and currently no Internet equivalent to telephone random digit dialing, researchers requiring data gathered from probability samples are best advised to consider other types of surveys. The nonprobability samples that can be selected quickly for Internet surveys work well for exploratory research or as part of a multimethod approach.

7. *Would multimedia or interactive features enhance the questionnaire?* Unlike paper questionnaires, online surveys may include streaming audio or video. Additionally, online questionnaires are arguably the most effective self-administered format for asking contingency questions. Web questionnaires can be programmed to avoid logical inconsistencies in follow-up questions. While programming errors may still exist, the automation of skip patterns eliminates the possibility of respondents answering the wrong questions—for example, participants who were not registered to vote responding that they had selected candidate "A" in a recent election.

8. *Does the researcher have the technical ability to create an online survey, or are there funds available to hire someone?* If the researcher does not have the technological knowledge or skills to create the survey online, then either a consultant must be included in the budget or another method should be employed. There are presently hundreds of commercial services available to aid researchers in the creation, distribution, and analysis of online surveys. These businesses vary greatly in the quality of customer service and data they provide as well as in their pricing structures.

Table 1.1 summarizes the advantages and disadvantages of conducting surveys via mail, by telephone, face-to-face, and online.

Online Survey Studies

Online survey research is still in the early stages of development; however, studies are beginning to reveal optimal ways to use this research method.

Table 1.1   Comparison of Survey Methods

Survey Type	Advantages	Disadvantages
Mail	• Low cost • Wide geographic reach • No interviewer bias • Anonymity allows sensitive questions	• Low response rate • Lengthy response period • Contingency questions not effective • Don't know who is responding to the survey
Telephone	• Limited coverage bias • Speedy responses • Can ask complex questions • Wide geographic reach	• Confusion with sales calls • Intrusive • Call screening • No visual support
Face-to-face interview	• Good response rates • Can ask complex questions • Long interviews tolerated	• Limited geographic reach • Time-consuming • Expensive • Interviewer bias • Sensitive topics difficult to explore
Online	• Low cost • Fast • Efficient • Contingency questions effective • Direct data entry • Wide geographic reach	• Coverage bias • Reliance on software • Don't know who is responding to the survey

These studies focus on response patterns and survey design. This brief review focuses on response rates and speed and data quality. Survey design is addressed in Chapter 5. Overall, the research indicates that when compared with mail surveys, online surveys' response rates are lower, response speed is higher, and data quality is the same or better. The lower response rate for e-mail surveys may be due to limited prior research on survey design; response rates are likely to increase as more research is conducted on designing online surveys and as diffusion of Internet technology increases in the general population.

Response Rates and Speed

In terms of response rate, the literature is divided into the two common types of online research: e-mail surveys and Web-based surveys. There is a wide range of response rates that are considered acceptable. In general, a response rate of 50% is adequate, a 60% response rate is good, and a 70% response rate is considered very good (Kittleson, 1997). Overall, the literature indicates that the response rates for e-mail surveys range between 24% and 76%. The response rates for Web-based surveys are approximately 30%, but the studies are limited in number. Table 1.2 shows a summary of the response rates and speed from mail surveys, e-mail surveys, and Web-based surveys.

Table 1.2   Response Rates and Speed for Mail, E-Mail, and Web-Based Surveys

Study	Response Rates (%)			Response Speed (days)	
	Mail	E-Mail	Web	Mail	Online
Bachmann, Elfrink, and Vazzana (1996)	65.6	52.5	a	11.18	4.68
Couper, Balir, and Triplett (1999)	70.7	42.6	a	a	a
Hamilton (2004)	a	a	32.52	a	<3
Kittleson (1997)	a	47.5	a	a	a
Kwak and Radler (2002)	42.5	a	27.4	9	2.2
Paolo, Bonaminio, Gibson, Partidge, and Kallail (2000)	41	24	a	40%[b]	100%[b]
Pearson and Levine (2003)	a	50.03	a	a	a
Schaefer and Dillman (1998)	57.5	58	a	14.39	9.16
Truell and Goss (2002)	57	36.1	a	24.2	12.5
Walsh, Kiesler, Sproul, and Hesses (1992)	a	76	a	a	a

a. Not measured.

b. After 2 weeks.

Data Quality

The quality of survey data can be evaluated in terms of item nonresponse and the amount of information obtained from **open-ended questions**. In general, the research indicates that the nonresponse rate in online surveys is lower than or similar to the rate in mail surveys and the number of words recorded for open-ended questions is higher in online surveys than in mail surveys. In a study that investigated word counts from open-ended questions on mail and Web-based surveys, Kawak and Radler (2002) found an average of 10.65 words on mail surveys and 15.56 words on Web-based surveys.

While much of the investigation concerning the best strategies for conducting online survey research remains to be undertaken, the research to date, along with our experience conducting online and traditional surveys, provides the basis for our recommendations in this text.

Summary

Although there is still a great deal to learn about online surveys, the research to date is valuable to the developers and researchers using this type of data collection tool. Online surveys are an effective way to gather information quickly and relatively inexpensively from a large geographic region. E-mail and Web-based surveys are useful in many situations; however, it is important to emphasize that they are not appropriate for all types of survey research. Researchers should carefully assess the target audience, research objectives, and data reporting needs when selecting a survey format.

2

Planning the Online Survey

A sound plan is essential to the success of any research endeavor. Survey research is a process, and each element has an impact on the others. Research objectives guide questionnaire format; questionnaire format determines the types of questions that may be used; the types of questions used determine data analysis; data analysis reflects research objectives; and all of this is bound by time, budget, and ethical considerations.

The first step in the planning process is to articulate a plan for the survey. This plan will be a handy map to which you can continually return as you address the individual components of the survey-planning process. These outlines are also particularly useful when the survey is part of a team research project.

In this chapter, we consider the major elements of a survey plan—namely, choosing an e-mail or a Web page survey, selecting survey software, writing clear project objectives, preparing timelines, and ethical considerations important in the online survey environment.

E-Mail Surveys

E-mail surveys are economical and fast to create. However, they are limited to simple questionnaires, whereas Web page surveys can include audio, video, complex branching patterns among the questions, and randomized questions. Although the use of e-mail is growing rapidly, it is not universal. According to a 2003 U.S. Census Special Study, 88% of adult Internet users use the Internet to send or receive e-mail. Many segments of the population, notably the elderly and the lower-income groups, do not have access to e-mail. It is therefore best to confine the use of e-mail surveys to professional, corporate, academic, or other environments where most members of the population are known to have e-mail access. The following are the specific advantages and disadvantages of e-mail surveys.

Advantages

- *Speed:* An e-mail questionnaire can be sent to hundreds or even thousands of people by entering or importing the distribution list and hitting the send key. It can gather thousands of responses within a day or two (McCullough, 1998).

- *Economy:* Creating e-mail surveys does not require survey software or the services of a **Web survey** host. Once the sample has been selected and the questionnaire drafted, there is practically no cost in administering the survey.

- *Convenience:* Having the questionnaire in the body of an e-mail message makes it easy for respondents to return the questionnaire by using the reply feature of their e-mail program.

- *Simplicity:* No special software or technical expertise is needed to conduct e-mail surveys. The developer only needs to be familiar with basic e-mail and word-processing programs.

Disadvantages

- *Availability of a sampling frame:* You must have access to a list of the population you wish to survey. If you do not have access to such a list, you must be able to purchase or compile one.

- *Technical limitations:* While it is possible to include graphic elements in an e-mail survey, this may create large file sizes that are often blocked by e-mail servers. For reasonable file sizes, it is best to limit e-mail questionnaires to text only.

- *Limited question types:* E-mail surveys cannot automatically skip or randomize questions.

- *Unsolicited e-mail (i.e., spam):* Many e-mail programs have filters to flag unsolicited messages as junk mail. Some filters will not accept bulk e-mails.

- *Data entry:* E-mail surveys require data entry before analysis.

- *Anonymity is not preserved:* The researcher will have the e-mail address of the person who responded to the e-mail and can link the responses to the respondent.

Internet/Intranet (Web Page) Surveys

Web surveys have many of the speed and convenience advantages of e-mail surveys plus added features that may make them a more practical option for researchers contemplating online surveys. However, taking advantage of these added features often means additional costs and the need for technical expertise. Consider the following advantages and disadvantages of Web-based surveys.

Advantages

- *Speed:* If posted on a popular Web site, a questionnaire has the potential to gather thousands of responses within hours.

- *Audience:* You can post the link on numerous Web sites with the permission and cooperation of the site's owner. This could broaden your audience as you could have the link located on sites whose audience consists of researchers, teachers, children, students, and so on.

- *Economy:* Web surveys are the most economical means by which to collect data from large numbers of respondents who may be geographically dispersed. After the initial set-up costs (software, Web hosting, etc.), it costs no more to target large samples than small ones. Moreover, direct data entry eliminates the need for data-entry personnel, thus further reducing costs.

- *Added content options:* Many Web survey hosts and software packages offer the facility to embed images and audio and video files. This may increase the time it takes for the Web page to load, so these options should be employed judiciously.

- *Expanded question types:* Web page questionnaires can include a wide variety of question types and can be programmed to skip questions when necessary, ensuring more accurate data than when respondents are asked to skip questions in an e-mail questionnaire.

- *The ability to ask sensitive questions:* Web surveys are similar to other forms of self-administered surveys in that there is no researcher present and participants complete the questionnaire at their own pace. This type of self-administered format has been shown to be optimal for inquiring about sensitive or embarrassing information (see Schaefer & Dillman, 1998).

• *Anonymity is preserved:* There is no e-mail address linked to a Web survey response.

Disadvantages

• *Limited populations:* Internet use is quickly becoming the norm in America, and the number of people using computers and accessing the Internet increases substantially each year. Even though there is some disagreement about the exact number of households online, one fact is clear: The online population does not reflect the general population of the United States. There is an upward bias in socioeconomic status among Internet users, and Web surfers are not evenly represented across ethnic groups. (See Tables 2.1 and 2.2 for details about the worldwide and American Internet populations.) This precludes the use of Internet surveys for projects aiming to draw conclusions about general populations.

• *Abandonment of the survey:* Respondents can easily quit in the middle of a questionnaire. To minimize the likelihood of respondents quitting, questionnaires should be as short as possible—that is, ask only the questions that are related to the project objectives. Avoid the temptation to add a few more questions because "you're conducting the survey anyway." It also helps if the questionnaire is easy to navigate and fun to complete. Pretesting the questionnaire will provide feedback about ease of navigation, and an understanding of the target population will aid in the inclusion of items that are interesting and relevant to the respondents. Offering incentives may help prevent abandonment of the survey.

• *Dependence on software:* Internet surveys require researchers to use software to create and deploy questionnaires. There are numerous choices of software packages and online survey companies. The products vary greatly in cost, ease of use, and flexibility. The novice may find the choices daunting. In the following section, we suggest some factors to consider when purchasing software.

What to Consider When Buying Survey Software and Selecting a Web Survey Host

To conduct a Web-based survey, you will need software and the services of a Web-based survey host. There are hundreds of commercial software programs and Web-based survey hosts on the market (see Appendix A).

Table 2.1   Internet Users Worldwide, 2002 and 2005

Country	2002 (%)	2005 (%)
The Netherlands	—	72
Great Britain	47	71
Canada	68	71
United States	64	70
Germany	47	60
France	41	57
Spain	—	53
Morocco	—	41
Poland	20	38
Lebanon	36	37
China	24	33
Turkey	18	32
Jordan	25	20
Russia	7	15
India	3	14
Indonesia	5	7
Pakistan	4	5

SOURCE: Data from Pew Reasearch Center. Used with permission.

NOTE: Data are based on the question "Do you ever go online to access the Internet or the World Wide Web or to send and receive e-mail?"

Table 2.2   Internet Use in the United States, June 2005

Characteristic	Percentage[a]
Age (years)	
18–29	84
30–49	80
50–64	67
65 and older	26
Race	
African American	57
White	70
Education	
Less than high school graduate	29
High school graduate/GED	61
College graduate	89

SOURCE: Based on data from Pew Research Center.

NOTE: a. Total percentage of American adults using Internet = 68. Data are based on telephone interviews with 2,001 adults living in the continental United States.

Web-based survey hosts (also known as application service providers [ASPs]) typically offer customers a full range of services, including the ability to create questionnaires, conduct surveys, analyze data, and produce and share reports, all via the company's Web site. Some Web survey companies offer the option of purchasing software that can be used locally on the researcher's computer; questionnaires are then uploaded to a Web site or e-mailed to respondents. This option leaves researchers responsible for installing the software and providing their own technical support for the system. Many of the ASPs (e.g., Zoomerang.com, SurveyMonkey.com) offer free trial versions of their services, and most software vendors have mini versions of their full packages available for customers to try.

There is a multitude of benefits that comes with using commercial software and Web-based survey hosts. The advantages include reduced development time and, hence, lower costs; a variety of design templates from which to choose; and the ability to compute basic statistics and the capability to export data to Excel or **SPSS** files for more complex data analysis. The challenge comes in selecting an appropriate software and online survey host for your needs and level of technical expertise. Although we won't evaluate specific vendors here, we will address some important considerations when choosing software and a survey host:

- *Expense:* Survey software and ASPs vary greatly in price. One company advertises downloadable survey software for a little more than $20.00; at the upper end of the range, we found a company that offered a custom software package plus Web hosting for approximately $16,000. The issue of cost is usually one of finding a product that contains the features you will actually use for the lowest price. Custom software packages may be appropriate if your needs are very specific (and your budget large); however, you may find that an off-the-shelf product may be adequate if your survey requires only basic features. Clearly, the $16,000 software will include many more options than the $20.00 version, but if you do not make use of those added features, they will slow down the questionnaire development process as you will have to navigate around them.

- *Ease of use:* Look for survey software that has an easy-to-use design interface with drag-and-drop capabilities for questions and scales, notes, and other text. **Wizards** that walk users through the survey creation process and questionnaire templates can be useful if you're new to using survey software. You also should be able to save a survey you create as a template so that you may use it again in the future. Question libraries also can be valuable for new survey researchers. These libraries typically include standard demographic and opinion items and can speed up the creation of the questionnaire.

- *Question number, formats, and **response options**:* Check for the capacity to ask a wide variety of questions using different response options. Question formats that should be included are single response, multiple responses, scale responses (i.e., agree-disagree; 1–5 points, etc.), and matrix responses. Other useful features allow developers to use radio buttons, check boxes, and open-text boxes and to randomize question order, which may be helpful for lengthy questionnaires that may result in respondent fatigue. It is also desirable to be able to choose whether respondents may be allowed to skip questions or whether answers will be forced before they are allowed to continue with the questionnaire. Forcing responses can lead to abandonment of the survey.

- *Contingency questions:* Contingency questions allow your respondents to be directed to a new set of questions on the basis of their responses. With online surveys, this means that participants are not forced to read and answer unnecessary questions. Also, look for a "skip-and-hit" option that can be based on respondent demographics or other criteria. For example, the president, accountant, and administrator of an organization can receive the same survey but be redirected to different sets of questions depending on their position.

- *Questionnaire options:* Less expensive software packages and ASPs sometimes limit the number of questions you can place on the questionnaire and the number of responses you can collect with any one survey. Other typical limitations include the inability to use tables, images, audio, video, and **ALT tags** on the survey. If you know you will be conducting simple surveys with small samples, these limitations may not pose a problem. If, however, you wish to expand to longer questionnaires or survey large samples of respondents, you will need to look for software without these limits.

- *Questionnaire appearance:* Evaluate the options for customizing questionnaires. Ask if the software allows you to include logos; also, ask about the available fonts and colors. If you will be surveying special populations such as children or the elderly, this is especially important as you will want to ensure that large font sizes are available. Also, inquire about the configuration of navigation and progress bars.

- *Sampling features:* If you do not have an e-mail distribution list, some Web survey hosts, such as Zoomerang, will generate a sample for you, for a fee. Look for the ability to select random, stratified, systematic, and cluster samples.

- *Distribution options:* Look for survey software that allows for different modes of survey delivery. Even if you are only interested in conducting online surveys, you may want the option of printing a paper copy of the questionnaires as an alternative for respondents who have disabilities or who prefer a hard copy.

- *Respondent lists:* Your survey software should allow you to import a respondent list from another software program or your e-mail address book. This reduces the time associated with manually entering the respondent data. You also should have the options of sending prenotification e-mails and thank-you e-mails.

- *Tracking respondents:* You may want to track who has responded or limit replies to one recipient. A higher response rate means less error; effective survey software offers the option of follow-up reminders to **nonrespondents**. Tracking these nonrespondents in the software application provides quick access for follow-up correspondence. In addition to tracking who replied, you also should be able to limit replies to one respondent. This is especially important for online surveys because you avoid skewing the data with multiple replies from one user. The use of **cookies**, Internet protocol addresses, and randomly generated codes should be potential options for limiting responses to prevent multiple replies from a single user.

- *Reporting and analysis options:* It is important to choose software that allows you to analyze your data and provides user-driven views of the results. How much data analysis you want to conduct online will vary according to your research purpose. Most survey software applications allow users to conduct descriptive analysis online and produce basic reports. For more complex analyses, look for software that provides the option of exporting data directly to a data analysis package like SPSS or **SAS**; at the very least, data should be easy to export to Excel for later importing to the statistical software package of your choice. For individuals and businesses involved in frequent online data collection and intricate data analysis, an all-inclusive package may be the appropriate solution; STATPAC, for example, offers a reasonably priced product that includes software to create e-mail and Web-based surveys and conduct basic and advanced statistical analysis (including analysis of open-ended survey questions) and free Web hosting of surveys.

- *Sharing results:* You may want to post your results on a Web site or share them with the respondents or an outside party. Many Web hosts give researchers the option to share results with others by providing a **URL** for a Web page containing the results. These programs allow survey developers to post the URL on a Web site so that viewers can see the real-time or final responses, depending on when you post the URL. The developer also has the option to allow respondents to see the results immediately after he or she has completed the survey.

- *Accessibility:* You may require a Web host that can create questionnaires in an accessible format for those with visual impairments. WebSurveyor, for example, can create surveys for respondents who use screen readers. Some Web hosts, such as Zoomerang, will translate a survey into 42 languages and, if necessary, translate the responses. This translation service is provided for an additional fee.

- *Accounts:* Some Web-based survey hosts provide only one password and user name for each account. Therefore, a company with 100 people and one account can have only one person logged onto the Web-based host at a time. Other Web-based hosts will provide more than one password and user name for the price of one account. If multiple members of the research team will need access to the Web host at the same time, it is important to investigate the vendor's account restrictions.

- *Survey security:* Password protection prevents unauthorized users from responding to the survey. Depending on the nature of the surveys you will be creating, this may be a necessary feature.

- *Customer support and training:* Be sure to evaluate the online help and customer support features of the survey software provider. Most applications come with help menus, and some are more helpful than others; it is advisable to test the software's help menus during the trial period. Also, look for toll-free customer service phone numbers, live online support, and on-site training options.

Survey Objectives

All research should begin with clarification of objectives. What are you trying to find out by conducting an online survey? The objectives of the project determine whom you will survey and what you will ask them. If your objectives are unclear, the results will probably be unclear. Commit to these goals in writing to help keep the survey focused. Make sure that you can tie in every questionnaire item to one or more of the survey's objectives.

Guidelines for Writing Survey Objectives

1. *Make objectives specific:* To write specific objectives, it is useful to start with a general goal statement that begins with the word *to* followed by

an action verb, such as *describe, explain, explore, identify, investigate, gauge, measure, assess*, or *test*—for example, "To investigate customer satisfaction levels." A list of specific objectives can then be generated from this goal statement. Example 2.1 shows a general research goal followed by a list of objectives. The level of specificity in the objectives will guide the researcher when writing questionnaire items.

Example 2.1

Goal: To assess credit union members' satisfaction with the current services

Objectives: To assess credit union members' satisfaction regarding the following:
   A. The waiting time to speak to a customer service representative
   B. The loan application process
   C. Membership fees
   D. Telephone banking services
   E. Checking account services
   F. Savings account services
   G. Bilingual services

Be sure that the survey objectives are in alignment with the format you choose to administer the survey; e-mail and Web-based surveys have innate coverage biases. For example, if your objective is to determine the satisfaction level of residents of the XYZ Retirement Village, then placing that survey on that village's Web site may not target the correct set of respondents. Evidence indicates that people aged 65 and older access the Internet less often than younger people. The Web site of a retirement village may be viewed more often by family members of the residents than the residents themselves.

2. *Write measurable objectives:* Whether an objective is measurable should be evaluated in light of the proposed survey format. Some objectives, such as those involving physiological variables, may very well be measurable but not in an online survey. Example 2.2 presents some measurable online survey objectives.

Example 2.2

   A. To assess students' opinions about the proposed mascot
   B. To determine the percentage of citizens who are likely to vote for Candidate A
   C. To determine employees' attitudes about the new delivery system
   D. To collect members' ratings of the workshop

---

3. *Have your objectives reviewed by experts:* There are two types of experts to consider: (a) content experts and (b) methodologists. Content experts have in-depth knowledge in specific areas. For example, if you're conducting an election study, you might seek out political scientists or sociologists with expertise in voting behavior. These individuals can offer advice about the topic of the survey and provide a context for the research. Methodologists, on the other hand, are experts in the survey process. They can help you create specific and measurable objectives and offer advice about the feasibility of achieving your objectives with an online survey.

4. *Review the literature related to your topic:* A literature review is a basic component of most academic research papers. Even if your project does not require a formal literature review, it is valuable to conduct one anyway. In doing so, you can learn from the work of others; specifically, you will see how others have formulated their research objectives and approached specific problems in the research process. In addition, you may find that the data you are seeking to collect already exist. There are numerous research consortiums and institutes that routinely collect a host of social data (e.g., the General Social Survey conducted by researchers at the University of Chicago) and make it available to member institutions and their constituents.

Survey Timelines

Timelines need not be complicated. They can be as simple as listing what you plan to accomplish each week. If there is an external project deadline, you will need to start from that deadline and work backward to the present. In this scenario, researchers often find that they need more time than is available. There is a couple of options for this situation: (a) limit the research objectives to only those that can be adequately addressed in the available time or (b) decrease the acceptable sample size, thereby reducing the amount of time the survey stays in the field. Note that by decreasing the sample size, you will increase the error associated with the statistical estimates obtained from the sample data. Example 2.3 gives a timeline showing the major steps in conducting an online survey research organized by week.

Example 2.3: Research Timeline

Week 1:   Write research objectives. Begin literature review.

Week 2:   Continue literature review. Have research objectives reviewed by experts.

Week 3:	Revise objectives. Decide between e-mail and Web-based survey administration.
Week 4:	Select survey software and Web host if using Web-based survey. Locate or compile sampling frame. Select sample or import e-mail list of potential respondents.
Week 5:	Prepare a draft of questionnaire online. Have experts review questionnaire for content and technical difficulties. Pretest questionnaire with sample of target respondents and experts in the field.
Week 6:	Revise questionnaire and test it again. Prepare survey invitations.
Week 7:	Deploy questionnaire. Monitor responses.
Week 8:	Continue to monitor responses. Send follow-up reminders to nonrespondents.
Week 9:	Process and analyze data.
Week 10:	Write first draft of research report.
Week 11:	Write second draft of research report. Prepare research presentation.
Week 12:	Complete research report and presentation.
Week 13:	Present research paper and results.

Obviously, timelines for research vary greatly depending on the nature of the project, the hours per week devoted to the research, the number of researchers involved, and the complexity of the data analysis required. The preceding example is intended to outline the major tasks to be accomplished and not to suggest time limits for the completion of each task.

Survey Research Ethics

Sometimes all the daily activities involved in conducting a research project cause us to forget about the "big picture" issues related to surveys. Survey researchers frequently encounter situations that are open to a variety of interpretations. Situations requiring an ethical interpretation are no different. Two individuals faced with an identical situation will likely perceive that situation in their own way and consider two different courses of action to be equally acceptable. As a result, organizations concerned with research (e.g., the American Psychological Association), and survey research in particular (e.g., the Council of American Survey Research Organizations), have developed guidelines outlining researchers' ethical responsibilities. These guidelines are much too lengthy and involved to review in detail here. We encourage researchers to visit the Web sites of the major survey research organizations for comprehensive information regarding survey research ethics (see our Resource Guide for Web addresses). We will discuss three of the major issues covered in most ethical guidelines: (a) informed consent, (b) ensuring respondent confidentiality and anonymity, and (c) ethical interpretation and reporting of results.

Informed Consent

In almost all cases, respondents to online surveys will be volunteers. To make an informed decision about participating in the research, volunteers should be briefed on (a) the general nature of the survey, especially if sensitive or potentially embarrassing information will be addressed; (b) the identity of the sponsor of the research; (c) how the data will be used; (d) the average length of time to complete the survey and if they will be contacted in the future with additional surveys; and (e) whether there are any risks involved in participating in the survey, such as asking respondents to disclose uncomfortable or embarrassing information.

This information can be provided in the e-mail survey invitation or as part of the introduction to the questionnaire. Institutional review boards (IRBs) generally do not require signed consent forms for participants in surveys; in fact, it would be nearly impossible to get signed consent forms in online surveys. If you believe that your survey may pose any physical or psychological threat to respondents, you should consult with the appropriate IRB representative at your institution to ensure that the research protocol includes appropriate safeguards to protect participants.

Confidentiality and Anonymity

Perhaps one of the most stringent requirements in all social research is maintaining the confidentiality of participants. Frequently, the respondents to your survey will expect that the information they provide will be confidential—that is, neither the fact of their participation nor the information they provide will be disclosed to third parties. If you have promised confidentiality, you have an ethical responsibility to ensure that participants' identification and information is protected. If you cannot (or will not) prevent the disclosure of respondent information, you must make this fact abundantly clear in the invitation to participate in the online survey so that respondents have the opportunity to refuse participation.

Often the promise of anonymity is included in the same sentence that guarantees confidentiality, almost as if the two concepts were the same. The statement typically reads "All your responses will remain strictly confidential and anonymous." Unfortunately, many people forget that anonymity extends beyond not requiring names and addresses on a questionnaire. Technically, responses to e-mail surveys are never truly anonymous, because researchers know the respondents' e-mail addresses. Even without this information, it is easy to attach identifying code numbers to questionnaires or to link survey numbers to databases containing respondent information. As a result, many potential respondents are skeptical of electronic surveys offering anonymity. The important fact here is not that researchers *must* promise anonymity. What is essential is that if the promise is made, the researcher is obligated to take the necessary steps to ensure that identifying information about survey respondents is kept separate from their responses.

Additionally, even if survey respondents know that their anonymity is not guaranteed (e.g., so that follow-up information can be gathered or so you can contact the respondent again in the future), you have a responsibility to the respondent to guarantee that subsequent contact is appropriate. For example, don't tell a potential respondent that he or she may be contacted to gather more information when you are really selling the name to a marketing company.

Survey Reporting and Interpretation

When reporting survey results, a host of situations arises that can potentially jeopardize respondent confidentiality and the accurate interpretation and presentation of research results.

When gathering demographic information that can identify respondents, the survey researcher has an obligation not to produce reports that can lead to the identification of individuals. For example, in an employee survey, it is reasonable to ask about gender and ethnic background to ensure that the needs of all employees are being met. If this information is gathered, be careful not to provide a report that can lead to the identification of individual employees. For example, when providing information at the department level, do not present the data so the only male, Hispanic employee can be identified. A reasonable rule of thumb to avoid this problem is to produce results only for groups containing at least 10 individuals. This way, no individual can be singled out.

Data interpretation can present another set of problematic issues for survey researchers. Efforts should be made to fully and accurately represent the results gathered by the survey. Too often, people do not present enough information about the procedures used for gathering the data, the sampling strategy, the error and confidence levels, the response rates, or how the data were analyzed. Without this information, it is easy to misinterpret the results or overinterpret some findings, which will lead to erroneous conclusions.

Another situation arises when researchers are asked not to report data that present the host organization in an unfavorable manner. As mentioned above, every effort should be made to present the results of the survey completely and accurately. This may mean presenting some information that suggests areas of discord or opportunities for improvement. These results should not be hidden or simply forgotten. Doing so is a disservice to the organization and the people who responded to the survey, not to mention questionable ethics.

Summary

In this chapter, we have addressed some foundational issues relevant to many online survey situations. Having considered the advantages and disadvantages of e-mail versus Web page surveys, features to look for in survey software packages, writing objectives and creating timelines, and a few key research ethics topics, we now proceed to sample selection and writing survey questions.

3

Sampling

I n this chapter, we examine the methods of selecting participants for Internet surveys. The decisions surrounding sample selection are critically important and should be considered in light of the survey objectives. For exploratory studies, convenience samples may be sufficient; when aiming to make statistical inferences about populations, however, it is necessary to employ a probability sampling technique. Before beginning our discussion of specific sampling procedures for online surveys, we will review some fundamental concepts related to sampling. Next, we will discuss the probability and nonprobability approaches that may be used in online surveys. Finally, we will consider the sources of error in online surveys.

Populations and Samples

In much of social research, investigators are interested in the opinions or attributes of the group of people who participate in the research because of what those individuals can tell them about the population from which they are selected. When a researcher writes objectives for a survey project, he or she already has a specific population in mind. A *population* is the entire group of individuals, groups, or objects to which you would like to generalize your research results—for example, citizens of a country, students at a university, or employees of a company. When you collect data on every member of a population, you are conducting a **census**. For many research projects, collecting census data is neither feasible nor practical. For example, say you are interested in determining the career plans of all college seniors in the United States. It would be impossible to conduct a census of this group. By the time you finish questioning each student, some might be nearing retirement age. As we will see shortly, however, online surveys may provide one of the few opportunities for conducting censuses in a reasonably timely manner.

Once the population has been identified, the next task is to find or generate a list of the population members. This list is called the *sampling frame*. Readily available sampling frames include e-mail distribution lists of employees of an organization, members of an association, or subscribers to a service.

With a sampling frame in hand, you are ready to draw your sample. A *sample* is a subset of the population. It consists of the group of people who are selected to participate in the research. Data are collected from sample participants to make conclusions about population characteristics. When we ask a group of 1,000 citizens about their opinions of a government policy, our real purpose is to make inferences about the population's opinions based on the data provided by the sample. A good sample is one that is representative of the population from which it is drawn.

Some Web survey hosts will, for a fee, generate a list of potential respondents that match your sampling frame. For example, Zoomerang will allow the researcher to select a variety of potential respondent attributes. These attributes include characteristics such as demographics (ethnicity, marital status, language spoken at home), geographic region, occupation, interests, and consumption (shopping, home and pet ownership, restaurant dining frequency).

The sample selected from the population is not necessarily the group that actually completes the research. For every sample selected, there will be individuals who are unreachable as well as *nonrespondents*: individuals who choose not to participate in the study. Even among the individuals who initially agree to participate, there will be **dropouts**: respondents who do not finish the questionnaire. We will address nonresponse error later in this chapter.

A final issue to consider before deciding on a sampling strategy is the **eligibility criteria** for participants in your research. Consider two elements of eligibility: (a) inclusion criteria, the characteristics that allow a potential respondent to participate, such as being an adult, a nonsmoker, or a registered voter, and (b) exclusion criteria, characteristics that prohibit an individual's participation, such as a language barrier or men in a study on women's health issues.

Sampling Techniques for Internet Surveys

Saturation Sampling

Saturation sampling is not a sampling technique per se but an attempt to conduct a population census. Recall from our earlier discussion that conducting a census, or collecting data on every member of a population, is an alternative, albeit an infrequently used one, to traditional survey sampling. The factors that usually render population censuses impossible—expense, timeliness, large population sizes, and inaccessibility—can largely be overcome in online surveys.

In an online survey, as opposed to telephonic or face-to-face interviewing, there is no difference in the expense or effort involved in sending an e-mail invitation to 10 or 10,000 members of an organization. Because online survey data have the benefit of being automatically posted to a database, there will be no added staff costs for data entry if thousands of questionnaires are returned. Moreover, the distribution of the questionnaires as well as the data analysis can be completed relatively quickly. Finally, the researcher opting for an online survey would do so only if the population of interest is accessible in an online environment.

This approach begins with a sampling frame containing e-mail addresses of every member of the target population. All members of the population are sent an e-mail invitation to participate, with appropriate measures taken to ensure that participants respond only once. (Commercial software programs send cookies to the respondent's computer to prevent them from responding more than once.) The questionnaire can be included in the body of the e-mail message or as an attachment, or the respondents can be directed to a Web page to complete the survey.

Saturation sampling is commonly used in settings such as universities, corporations, government agencies, and professional associations. Using this technique eliminates coverage error, because every member of the population is invited to participate in the survey. Although coverage error is not an issue when using saturation sampling, nonresponse error remains a concern. Researchers can, however, compute response rate (because the number of potential respondents receiving invitations is known) and take steps to increase participation. Some examples of the use of saturation sampling can be found in Example 3.1.

Example 3.1

- A university sends out an e-mail invitation to all students, faculty, and staff to participate in an opinion survey about a proposed name change.

- A health management organization e-mails all participating physicians to collect data about the new patient referral system.
- The human resources department of a corporation e-mails all managers asking them to participate in a Web page survey about improving employee performance reviews.

Probability Sampling

The traditional classification of survey sampling methods into probability and nonprobability techniques is useful for Internet surveys. Probability samples are those for which the probability of each participant's inclusion can be computed. These samples depend on random selection of participants from a defined sampling frame and afford the researcher the opportunity to make conclusions about population characteristics based on sample statistics. Table 3.1 shows the probability and nonprobability samples that may be used in online surveys.

Table 3.1   Types of Probability and Nonprobability Samples for Online Surveys

Probability Samples	*Nonprobability Samples*
For closed populations	Convenience
Simple random	Volunteer opt-in panel
Systematic	Snowball
Stratified	
Cluster	
For open populations	
Intercept	
Pre-recruited panel	

Random Sampling From a Closed Population

With a comprehensive sampling frame, such as an employee or a membership list, it is possible to employ a random sampling technique to select potential survey respondents. Even if the list does not contain e-mail addresses, it may still be possible to select a random sample by inviting respondents, via telephone or postal mail, to participate in the survey. To select a random sample of participants from a closed population, first secure (or create) the sampling frame, then select a simple random sample, a systematic random sample, a stratified sample, or a cluster sample. (See Appendix B for a review of these probability sampling techniques.)

Probability Sampling From an Open Population

Open populations are those for which there is no readily available sampling frame—for example, residents of a city. Selecting a probability sample of these individuals is considerably more challenging than in a closed population. Currently, the only way to achieve a truly random sample of an open population is to employ a multimethod approach, such as contacting respondents by phone (using a random digit dialing protocol) and inviting them to log on to a Web site to participate in the survey. Although, the benefit of speed associated with Internet surveys will be lost, the researcher can take advantage of other online survey features such as the ability to present still images and video and direct data entry.

The multimethod approach that creates pre-recruited panels of respondents and a technique that restricts the population of interest to visitors to particular Web sites are two methods currently being used to select probability samples from open populations.

Pre-Recruited Panels. A pre-recruited panel is a group of survey respondents who are recruited by a variety of methods (e.g., e-mail solicitation, telephone random digit dialing, mail invitations, and face-to-face interviews) and who agree to be available for repeated survey participation. Participants are selected randomly from the panel and are sent invitations to participate in particular surveys.

The California-based company Knowledge Networks (www.knowledgenet works.com) claims to maintain the only Internet panel that represents the full spectrum of Internet and non-Internet households. Their panel consists of more than 40,000 participants who were randomly recruited by telephone (using random digit dialing). Households that did not have Internet access were provided with hardware and free Web access.

Nonresponse, while still an issue, is generally lower in pre-recruited panels than in other samples, because the participants have previously agreed to participate. The nonresponse rate can be computed and nonrespondents evaluated. In other words, because researchers have demographic information about all panel participants, it is possible to test for systematic biases among nonrespondents that may limit the study's generalizability.

Another concern is the creation of "professional survey respondents"—individuals who become proficient at answering questionnaires based on familiarity with online surveys rather than the actual questions. When using a pre-recruited panel, the frequency of respondent participation should be limited to minimize this risk.

Intercept Sampling. This procedure uses pop-up windows to invite respondents to participate in the survey. Web survey software can be programmed to issue pop-up invitations randomly or systematically, say for every nth visitor to the Web site. This is an intrusive approach and is often accompanied by an incentive for participation. The sampling frame is limited to visitors to the particular Web site; therefore, generalizations to broader populations must be made with caution. Nonresponse is also a concern, hence the accompanying incentives. Intercept sampling can be effective in certain situations—for example, customer satisfaction surveys for an online merchant.

Margin of Error and Confidence Level for Surveys Conducted With Probability Samples

When we say that the results of a survey are precise, we mean that our estimates are correct to within a small margin of variability. To illustrate, we will consider an example of estimating a *population proportion* based on a *sample statistic* when the sample is selected using a probability method. For most opinion polls, we can usually tolerate a **margin of error** of a few percentage points around the estimated percentage of the population who have a certain opinion, provided that we have a high level of confidence in this estimate. For example, say that you are conducting a survey aimed at determining citizens' opinions about a new zoning ordinance. If you come within five percentage points of the true percentage of those who feel a certain way (favor or oppose) and are 95% confident of this result, you would probably be satisfied. On the other hand, if you were conducting a survey just before a major election, you would want to be more precise, perhaps getting within 3% of the true proportion of the population who favor a particular candidate. This concept is called the margin of error.

How well a sample represents a population is gauged by both the margin of error and the *level of confidence.* For example, a public opinion survey question may have a margin of error of ± 3% at a 95% confidence level. This means that if the survey were conducted 100 times, the true percentage would be within 3 percentage points of the sample percentage in about 95 of the 100 surveys. If you find that in a random sample, 50% of the residents of a city favor a bond measure and your confidence level is 95% with a margin of error of 3%, you're saying that you're 95% confident that the true percentage of the population who favor the bond measure is between 47% and 53%.

The margin of error is related to sample size (the number of respondents) and is commonly reported at one of two levels of confidence: The 99% level is the most conservative, while the 95% level is the most frequently used.

Keep in mind that the margin of error tells you only about sampling error and is meaningful only if you are using a probability sample. It does not take into account other potential sources of error such as coverage error, non-response error, and bias in the question wording.

Sample Size

As sample size increases, margin of error decreases for a particular level of confidence. Table 3.2 provides the sample sizes necessary to guarantee a given margin of error for a given degree of confidence when using data from a simple random sample to estimate a population proportion (or percentage). At the 95% confidence level, a sample size of 384 will guarantee a maximum 5% margin of error when estimating a proportion; when the sample size is increased to 600, the margin of error will be no greater than 4%, and when it is increased to 1,067, the margin of error will be no greater than 3%. Although continuing to increase the sample size yields lower margins of error, there are diminishing returns. You would have to select a sample of more than 9,000 individuals to report findings at the 95% confidence level with 1% margin of error.

Table 3.2   Sample Sizes for Estimating a Population Proportion With Various Levels of Confidence and Margins of Error

Margin of Error (%)	90% Confidence Level	95% Confidence Level	99% Confidence Level
±5	272	384	666
±4	425	600	1,040
±3	756	1,067	1,849
±2	1,702	2,401	4,160
±1	6,806	9,604	16,641

NOTE: Assumes a simple random sample.

Table 3.2 serves as a guideline for determining the sample size you'll need for a particular amount of sampling error that you're willing to tolerate when estimating a population proportion with the sample statistic obtained from a simple random sample. It is important to note that if your analysis plan includes evaluating subgroups of the sample (e.g., different age groups or ethnicities), a larger sample may be necessary, because the margin of error for each subgroup is determined by the number of respondents in that group.

Nonprobability Sampling

Nonprobability samples do not employ random selection procedures and thus may or may not represent the population well. This is why most statistical texts advise against using nonprobability techniques or suggest that they be reserved for exploratory research. While this advice is theoretically sound, in online survey research it is often impractical. Hence, we present three nonprobability strategies that can be used for online surveys: convenience sampling, volunteer opt-in panels, and snowball sampling. The appropriateness of the chosen sampling method should be evaluated in light of the research objectives. In all cases, researchers using nonprobability sampling should refrain from making inferences about population characteristics based on sample data.

Convenience Sampling

Convenience sampling is a nonsystematic approach to recruiting respondents that allows potential participants to self-select into the sample. There are neither restrictions to participation nor controls over multiple submissions by a single respondent. The questionnaire is posted on the Web site for anyone to fill out. Examples of this sampling strategy can be found on news Web sites that conduct "question of the day" polls. There is also a growing number of Web sites dedicated to hosting Web polls (e.g., www.survey.net, www.misterpoll.com). Another convenience sampling strategy involves posting survey invitations on online community bulletin boards, discussion forums, and chat rooms. It should be noted, however, that many members of online communities find this practice inappropriate, offensive, and a violation of their privacy.

Convenience sampling requires less time and effort than generating probability samples. However, statistical inference is problematic. Respondents who self-select into Web polls are not representative of any underlying population; they tend to be individuals who have a particular interest in the survey topic. As Couper (2000) noted, the Web poll and its counterpart the 1-900 call-in poll have their place, namely, as entertainment. Online polls employing convenience samples should not be presented as legitimate scientific research.

Volunteer Opt-In Panels

The volunteer panel relies on assembling a group of individuals who have volunteered to participate in future surveys. Individuals are recruited via some form of advertising (usually Web based), and demographic information is collected when participants register. Panel members are selected (by convenience, quota, or random sampling) to receive a questionnaire, and steps are taken to ensure that participants respond only once. Two well-known examples of organizations using volunteer opt-in panels are the Harris Poll Online (www.harrispollonline.com) and Greenfield Online (www.greenfield.com). Both organizations point to their large and geographically dispersed panels as major benefits and claim that with the proper statistical corrections, their samples accurately represent various populations of interest.

The volunteer opt-in panel should not be confused with the pre-recruited panel. Members of the volunteer opt-in panel respond to advertisements and sign up to participate in the panel. Participants in pre-recruited panels are randomly selected from the online and offline populations and invited to participate on the panel; individuals who were not randomly selected are not permitted to volunteer for the panel.

To use a volunteer opt-in panel, researchers have the option of posting an ad on a Web site inviting volunteers to participate or using a commercial service that "sells" samples of volunteer respondents.

Snowball Sampling

The snowball sample begins by identifying one participant who meets your inclusion criteria. This first individual is then asked to refer someone else for the survey; then, you ask this second individual to refer someone else, and so on. This method is commonly used when dealing with hard-to-reach populations, such as citizens who may be reluctant to participate in surveys. Snowball sampling works best with small populations where the members know each other. While hardly representative of any general population, snowball sampling can be a good way to select members of specifically defined, highly targeted populations.

Sample Size for Nonprobability Samples

One of the most common questions associated with any type of survey sampling is how many elements of the population should be sampled. Statistical theory provides us with specific procedures for estimating the number of respondents necessary to make population inferences with various levels of confidence when we employ probability samples. As we have seen, these formulas are based on the particular probability sampling procedure used and the amount of sampling error we're willing to tolerate (Table 3.2 is the result of employing such a formula for simple random samples). No formulas for statistical inference exist for estimating sample size when using nonprobability samples. This is because in a nonprobability sample it is impossible to know the likelihood of any particular participant being selected for the sample; therefore, there is no estimate of the variability in the underlying population—essential information for the calculation of a suitable sample size.

Some of the answers that have been proffered in response to the question about how large a nonprobability sample should be include "large enough," "as big as your budget will allow," and "as large as it can be given your time frame." These answers are unsatisfying and offer little guidance to investigators involved in applied research. In an attempt to offer more concrete guidelines, survey methodologists grappling with this issue have suggested the following rules of thumb, which may be useful for researchers engaged in online research with nonprobability samples (Alreck & Settle, 1995; Hill, 1998):

- There is seldom justification for sample sizes less than 30 or larger than 500.
- Within the limits of 30 to 500, select a sample of about 10% of the parent population.
- When samples are to be broken into subsamples, the rules of thumb for samples sizes should apply to the subsamples.
- In multivariate research, sample size should be at least 10 times larger than the number of variables being studied.
- Generally, larger samples are better than smaller ones; select the largest sample that you can afford.

Although it is not specifically related to online survey research, Martin and Bateson (1986) suggested a method for checking the adequacy of one's sample that may be useful for Internet surveys: the split-half analysis for consistency. The procedure involves randomly dividing the sample into two halves and analyzing them separately. If the two sets of data are consistent, then you've collected enough data; if the conclusions differ, more data are needed.

Sampling in online surveys can be a thorny problem. Time and budget constraints typically lead researchers to settle for smaller samples than originally desired, and technical restrictions often prohibit the selection of the preferred simple random sample. This limits the generalizability of the research findings and may call the **reliability** of the data into question. Should survey researchers who are limited to the use of nonprobability samples just give up? In response to this query, Hill (1998) noted that it is better to have collected some data and gained some insight than to have collected no data and gained no information. We agree but hasten to add that researchers should exercise caution when making inferences about populations when results are based on nonprobability samples of any size. Finally, it is essential to keep in mind that the most important characteristic of *any* sample is that it be representative of the population from which it is drawn.

Sources of Error in Online Surveys

Coverage Error

Coverage error occurs when the sampling frame does not completely represent the population of interest. It is a function of the proportion of the population not covered by the sampling frame and the difference between the characteristics of respondents and nonrespondents (see Couper, 2000; Groves, 1989).

Estimates of household access to the Internet vary greatly. Household Internet penetration is growing rapidly, but the online population still differs from the general population in many ways, and there is wide variation in Internet access among subgroups in the population (see Chapter 2 for a breakdown of Internet use in the United States). However, there are segments of the populations where connectivity is almost universal. Some universities, for example, routinely assign all students and faculty e-mail addresses. Attempting to draw a probability sample for a Web survey is best done for populations that are narrowly defined and can be exhaustively represented by a sampling frame.

Nonresponse Error

Whereas coverage error exists when members of the population have no chance of being included in the sample, nonresponse error is a function of selected respondents choosing not to participate in the survey. The error can take two forms: *unit nonresponse*, when the respondent does not participate in the survey at all, and *item nonresponse*, when the respondent skips particular questions on the questionnaire. Unit nonresponse is calculated by dividing the number of individuals who fail to respond by the total number of potential participants invited to complete the survey. To determine nonresponse (or response rate), the denominator (those eligible to participate) must be known.

Item nonresponse can be evaluated by conducting item analyses of all survey questions. The descriptive statistics associated with each question should be analyzed, paying particular attention to the number of missing cases on each item. If you find that a large number of respondents skipped a particular question, then that question should be reviewed for clarity and proper functioning (i.e., perhaps there was a software error).

Nonresponse is a problem to the extent that those who choose not to participate are systematically different from those who choose to complete the survey. If the decision to participate (or not) were random, then nonresponse would not be an issue. The research literature surrounding nonresponse in Internet surveys is not as well developed as it is for mail and telephone surveys. In telephone surveys, for example, the literature tells us that socioeconomic status, suspicion about telemarketing calls, and interviewer skill are important factors influencing participation. Knowing this, we can employ strategies to compensate for nonresponse in those settings.

The emerging body of knowledge about nonresponse in Internet surveys is currently centered on response rates in e-mail surveys. Couper (2000) outlined three sets of explanations for the low response rates in Internet surveys: (a) the motivation tools used in mail or phone surveys cannot be used the same way in online surveys, and analogous instruments have not yet been developed; (b) technical difficulties may prevent some respondents from starting to answer questionnaires or cause them to abandon the survey halfway; and (c) concerns about the confidentiality of e-mail responses discourage some prospective participants.

While the field of research surrounding nonresponse in online surveys matures, we can use the existing literature as a basis for suggesting some techniques for improving the response rate in online surveys:[1]

- Include appeals to respondents' self-interest in survey invitations. Point out how they can "make a difference" by taking part in the survey. If appropriate, you also might note that important decisions will be made based on the survey data.
- Keep questionnaires as simple as possible so that they load quickly and without error on Web browsers.
- Remind respondents that their responses will be kept confidential. This is especially important in e-mail surveys, where anonymity is lost.

Sampling Error

Sampling error occurs when statistical estimates are made based on sample data rather than population data. The particular sample selected for a survey is only one of a number of possible samples that could have been selected. The estimates (e.g., **means** or proportions) from each sample can therefore vary from sample to sample just due to chance. When using a probability sample, chance variability in sample estimates can be measured by *standard errors* of estimates associated with a particular survey.

So why sample from populations? As we noted earlier in this chapter, the effort required to invite all members of a closed population to participate in an online survey is minimal. If you invited all 12,000 students at a university, for example, to take part in a survey, then you would have no sampling error, assuming that you weren't using these data to make inferences about students at other universities. Of course, you would still have to contend with nonresponse error. A problem is that if you plan to conduct multiple surveys with the same population, you will quickly burn out your respondents. Sampling allows you to repeatedly survey the same population without continually contacting the same individuals.

Summary

In this chapter, we have reviewed some of the basic concepts relevant to online survey sampling, discussed a variety of probability and nonprobability techniques for selecting a sample, and presented the sources of error associated with sampling. Survey sampling is complex, and we have barely scratched the surface of the topic. Readers interested in a more complete treatment should consult one of the many excellent books on sampling—for example, Scheaffer, Mendenhall, and Ott (2006); Levy and Lemeshow (1999); or the classic text by Kish (reprinted in 1995).

Note

1. Techniques for improving the response rate also are addressed in Chapter 6 of this volume.

4

Writing Survey Questions

A survey question is a measurement tool, a way for researchers to discover a respondent's opinion, knowledge, and behavior. Properly constructed questions are essential to any survey, and all good survey questions share some common characteristics. The best questionnaire items are short, unambiguous, and meaningful to the respondent. Poorly written questions, those that are lengthy or **double-barreled**, for instance, confuse and frustrate participants, often resulting in increased nonresponse. In this chapter, we cover the basics of writing effective survey questions. We start with some general considerations and a discussion about creating valid questions. We then discuss the distinction between open-ended and **closed-ended questions**; the types of closed-ended questions; the level of measurement; and the writing of questions to collect factual, demographic, and attitude data.

General Considerations

Every question you ask should be related to the survey's objectives. As you write each question, refer to your survey plan to confirm that the question does indeed address one or more of your research objectives. If you find that you've written a question that is not obviously related to one of your objectives, ask yourself what you intend to do with the data collected from the question. This is the time to revisit your survey plan and either revise your objectives or delete the question. Resist the urge to add questions simply because you're conducting the survey anyway. Not only will you needlessly lengthen the questionnaire, you'll also risk confusing respondents, because your questionnaire will lack coherence.

Online surveys are similar to self-administered paper-and-pencil question-naires. In both formats, respondents complete the survey in their environ-ment, at their own pace, and without the help (or hindrance) of the researcher. If you've ever written questions for a traditional self-administered question-naire, many of the guidelines for online survey questions will be familiar to you. For example, questions must be self-explanatory, easy to understand and answer, free of jargon, and visually appealing. Online surveys have the added capacity for including graphics and audio and video content, greatly increas-ing the type and format of data that can be collected. The most important dis-tinction between Internet surveys and other self-administered questionnaires is the ability to effectively ask contingency questions, that is, to automatically skip questions that are irrelevant to some respondents. Internet surveys can easily be programmed so that, for example, men and women are asked differ-ent sets of questions. We will discuss contingency questions shortly, but first we address some foundational issues surrounding measurement.

Validity of Measurement

Survey questions are valid to the extent that they measure the underlying concepts being investigated. A questionnaire item isn't valid or invalid per se; the **validity** of a measure can be evaluated only by examining the connec-tion between the question and the attitude, behavior, or fact that it purports to measure. Put simply, valid questions measure what they're supposed to measure. For example, if you wanted to know about respondents' magazine-reading habits, it would not make sense to ask how many magazine sub-scriptions they have. Purchasing a magazine subscription is not a valid indicator of magazine *reading*. Many people purchase magazines and never read them, while others read magazines without ever paying for them. It would be more valid to ask directly about the amount of time spent reading magazines. Validity refers to the link between individual questions and the concepts they seek to measure as well as to how groups of questions com-bine to measure multidimensional concepts.

Respondent-Centered Threats to Validity

There are several reasons why research participants may provide inaccurate information on a survey. They may deliberately report misinformation to avoid being embarrassed or to fit in with what they believe is the social norm for the situation. They may not have access to the information—for exam-ple, when asked about details, which may be difficult to recall. And, finally, respondents may offer opinions on surveys simply because someone is asking them for an opinion, not because they really have one.

Social Desirability

Social desirability, and its cousin political correctness, can often lead respondents to give the "right" answer rather than the real or valid answer to a survey question. The desire to conform to social norms can be powerful. This is why more people say they vote, go to museums and libraries, do volunteer work, and give money to charities than is actually the case. Social desirability bias is more of a problem in interview surveys than in self-administered formats. People generally give more honest answers when faced with a computer screen than when faced with an interviewer (even if the interview is on the telephone). This is not to suggest, however, that online surveys are immune from the problems created by individuals' desire to be viewed in a positive light. It is therefore useful to review some techniques for reducing social desirability bias.

Ways to Reduce Social Desirability Bias

- Repeat the promise of anonymity and confidentiality (that is, if it was given in the first place).

  Example 4.1: "Remember all of your responses are anonymous and will be kept confidential."

- Employ face-saving strategies, such as giving respondents permission to behave in socially unacceptable ways.

  Example 4.2: "Everyone gets angry now and then. How many times last week did you find yourself getting angry?"

- State that the behavior you're asking about is not unusual.

  Example 4.3: "A recent study found that 80% of college students have cheated on an exam. Have you ever cheated on an exam?"

Inaccurate Estimates

When survey respondents provide information about past behavior or events, they are almost always reporting an estimate rather than a precise value. For example, if asked how many hours of television they watched per day, most people would have to guess. The key to valid measurement of factual information is to ask respondents focused questions covering a limited range of time and situations. There are several reasons why participants may provide inaccurate estimates: They may not understand the parameters of the question, they may not be qualified to answer the question, or the question may ask about distant behaviors or events that are no longer salient.

Ways to Improve Accuracy of Estimates

- Ask about specific behavior within a limited, recent time period.

Example 4.4

Poor: "How many miles have you driven since you received your driver's license?"

Better: "How many miles did you drive last week?"

- Ask respondents about their own behavior, not the behavior of others.

Example 4.5

Poor: "What is your wife's favorite sport to watch on TV?"

Better: "What is your favorite sport to watch on TV?"

Example 4.6

Poor: "What is your annual household income?"

Better: "To the nearest $1,000, what is your annual income?"

- Ask respondents to think about a specific event rather than a category of events.

Example 4.7

Poor: "In an average week, how much do you spend on groceries?"

Better: "How much did you spend on groceries last week?"

Nonattitudes

Not every issue that is important to you will be important to the participants in your survey. You should ask yourself, "Is this topic one about which respondents have genuine opinions?" Several factors may account for why respondents sometimes answer opinion questions when, in fact, they have no opinion about the issue. First, few people want to admit to being uninformed; second, they would like to be viewed positively (i.e., social desirability bias); and finally, respondents may feel the need to "help" the researcher by completing all of the questionnaire items.

- Make it socially acceptable for respondents to say they are unfamiliar with the topic.

  Example 4.8: "Some people are interested in politics and some are not . . . would you say you are interested in national politics?"

- Use *screening* or *filter* questions.

  Example 4.9

   "Do you have an opinion about Proposition 101?"

   "Have you thought much about Proposition 101?"

- Provide an explicit "no opinion" choice as a response option.

  Example 4.10: "Should slot machines be allowed in card rooms?"

  Strongly Agree   Agree   No opinion   Disagree   Strongly Disagree

  ---

Question Format and Wording

We have seen that the validity of a questionnaire response may be compromised in three ways: (1) if respondents feel pressure to respond in socially desirable ways, (2) if respondents do not have or cannot accurately estimate the information being requested, and (3) if respondents do not have opinions on topics they're being asked about.

Validity, and the related concept of reliability or consistency of measurement, also can be threatened when the wording of survey questions is faulty or when questions contain inadequate or inappropriate response options. We will now proceed with a discussion of the two main categories of survey questions, open-ended and closed-ended, paying particular attention to techniques for writing questions that will elicit valid and reliable responses.

Question Formats

Open-Ended Questions

Open-ended questions are those for which response options are not provided. These questions allow participants to answer in their own words by typing their response into an empty text box (see Figure 4.1). They are particularly useful when investigating new topics and offer an opportunity to learn unexpected information. Conventional wisdom dictates that open-ended questions should be used sparingly in interview surveys and not at all on self-administered questionnaires. The reasoning is that respondents are turned off by the difficulty of being forced to recall and articulate information and will usually skip open-ended items when they can.

It is reasonable to assume that the same advice would hold for online surveys; after all, it is easier to click on a mouse than to type in a response. Research on Internet surveys provides important insight into respondent behavior with respect to open-ended questions. In a comparison of surveys distributed by e-mail and by postal mail, Schaefer and Dillman (1998) found that respondents were significantly more likely to answer open-ended questions in

Credit Union Survey

1. What do you like BEST about your bank?

2. What do you like LEAST about your bank?

Next >>

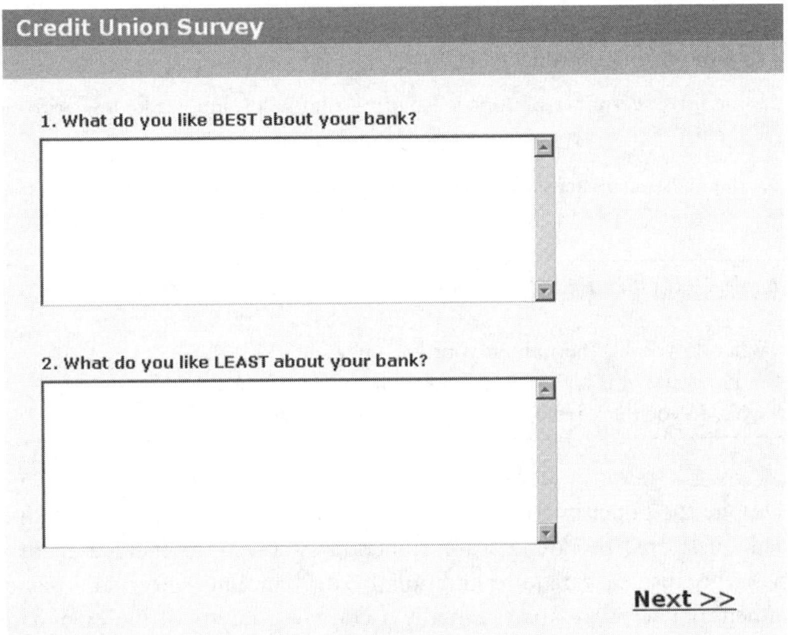

Figure 4.1   Open-Ended Question Example

the e-mail questionnaire than the mail version and the e-mail responses were significantly longer than the mail responses. Couper, Traugott, and Lamias (2001) found that while item nonresponse was indeed higher for questions with open text boxes than for those with a list of options, the responses that were provided tended to have a high degree of validity. Reja, Lozar Manfreda, Hlebec, and Vehovar (2003) also discovered that open-ended questions yielded more missing data than the same questions asked in a closed-ended format; however, the open-ended questions produced a more diverse set of answers.

Greater length and variety of answers to open-ended questions do not necessarily indicate that the answers are better than those collected via closed-ended questions. These findings do suggest, however, that the information obtained from open-ended questions on Internet surveys is similar to that from traditional survey methods in terms of validity. Open-ended questions tend to result in more valid responses than closed-ended questions because respondents are not forced to select from a list of response options created by the researcher.

Although information about the usefulness of open-ended questions on Internet surveys is now emerging, we can make some general recommendations. Use open-ended questions when

1. exploring new or unfamiliar topics;

2. the list of response options is lengthy—that is, it would take longer to read the list than to type in a response; and

3. the question elicits short answers: a few words, a phrase, or a brief sentence.

Example 4.11: Open-Ended Questions

- "What do you like best about your local newspaper?"
- "What would you say is the main reason you voted for Bates?"
- "What do you think is the most important problem in your community?"

Despite the potential to collect valid and detailed information with open-ended questions, researchers are sometimes reticent to include them on surveys because they require additional data handling before analysis can commence. The process is essentially a content analysis of the open-ended responses. Example 4.12 displays a portion of output showing responses to an open-ended question from an online voting survey.

Example 4.12

Why did you vote for Pam Jones?

1. Because she's a woman.
2. I like her positions on the issues and think she'll do the best job for our city; I especially like that she's an outsider and doesn't have ties to the corrupt members of the current council.
3. Don't know . . . she just seems like a nice lady.
4. I met her at a community open house and liked the way she presented herself. She answered questions honestly and wasn't afraid to say that she didn't know the answers to some of the questions that people asked her. She stands for the values I stand for and I think she'll be a good city council member.
5. Best of the bunch.
6. Because of her position on the development of the Lakeview area.
7. She's a working mom and I can relate to that.
8. Her position on the issues plus her personal qualities—like she's smart and honest.
9. Her campaign platform.
10. She has good plans for our city, including her ideas about the Lakeview district; her positions on the other issues that are important in my neighborhood; her integrity and family values.

The researcher would look at a sample of the responses and perhaps devise coding categories for the reasons for voting: (1) issue positions, (2) personal qualities, (3) plans for the city, and so on. Coders would then read through each of the open-ended responses and decide into which category to place the individual responses. The procedure typically involves two coders so that a measure of intercoder reliability (agreement between the two coders) can be computed. Clearly, this additional work requires time and resources and does not lend itself to fast turnaround of survey results. The benefit is that the coding categories are created based on participants' responses rather than created a priori based on the researcher's decisions, thus increasing the validity of the data.

For large data sets, hand coding of open-ended responses is prohibitively expensive and time-consuming. There are some software applications that can hasten the process; two notable examples are SPSS's Verbastat and STATPAC's Verbatim Blaster. The procedure is basically the same for both programs: Raw data from the Web survey application must be downloaded and then imported into Verbastat or Verbatim Blaster. The software searches the survey responses and counts unique words that appear in the text. Variations of the same word (e.g., plurals, different tenses, prefixes, and suffixes) are combined into a single root word. The result is a list of root words and the number of respondents who used each one (see Figure 4.2). The researcher then reviews the list and makes decisions about which words are "important." Those key terms are then carried forward into the second stage of the analysis, where the actual open-ended responses for each respondent are reviewed by the researcher; he or she can choose to accept the code category suggested by the software, select another category from a list, or create a new category (see Figure 4.3).

Verbastat is the more expensive of the two programs and is fully compatible with some Web survey development tools, such as SurveyCrafter and mrInterview. It is used by market research companies that routinely analyze a large volume of open-ended survey questions. Verbatim Blaster is included with STATPAC's basic statistics package and is a natural choice for researchers who are already using STATPAC's online survey development software.

Although programs like these, and other text-mining software, reduce the time it takes to process open-ended responses by initially searching text and

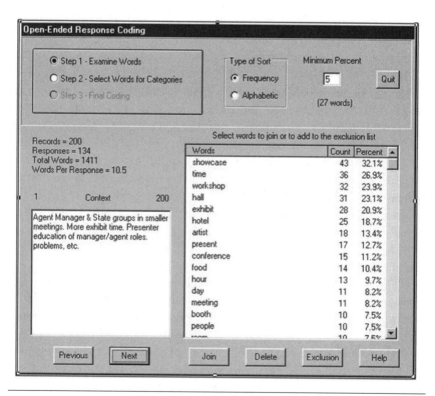

Figure 4.2   Verbatim Blaster Precoding Frame

SOURCE: Reprinted with permission of StatPac.

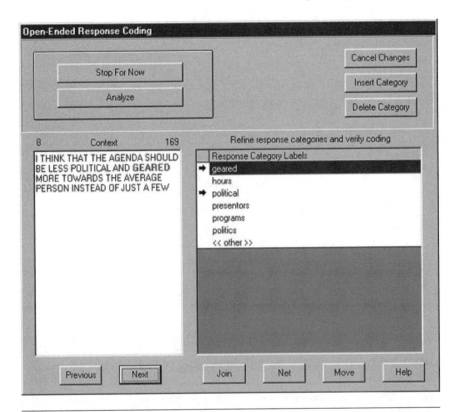

Figure 4.3 Verbatim Blaster Final Coding Frame

SOURCE: Reprinted with permission of StatPac.

creating coding categories, there is still a substantial amount of human labor involved in verifying the coding categories and reviewing the individual responses.

Close-Ended Questions

Closed-ended questions provide respondents with a list of response options from which to choose. These questions typically make up the bulk of most online questionnaires because they are easy to answer, are familiar to most respondents, and provide reliable measurement. The list of response options for closed-ended questions must be exhaustive—that is, cover all possible response options. Additionally, the items on the list should be mutually exclusive: A respondent should not be able to select more that one category at a time. Formats for closed-ended questions include dichotomous, multiple choice, rankings, and rating scales.

Dichotomous Questions. Dichotomous questions are those that present two possible response options—for example, yes/no; male/female.

Example 4.13

Are you registered to vote in Alameda County?

☐ Yes   ☐ No   ☐ Don't know

Do you own a cell phone?

☐ Yes   ☐ No

What is your gender?

☐ Male   ☐ Female

Even though the first question in Example 4.13 contains the "don't know" option, it is considered a dichotomous question. Note that the second and third questions in the example do not offer "don't know" as a choice. There are different schools of thought with respect to providing the "don't know" option on survey questionnaires. Some researchers choose not to include it as they believe it offers some respondents an easy way to avoid thinking about and answering the question. Others include the "don't know" option claiming that it provides valid data, because some respondents really may not know the answer.

As a rule of thumb, if it is reasonable to expect that respondents may not have the answer to a question—for example, on knowledge-based items—then include "don't know" as an option. If it seems, however, that most respondents should know the answer—as in the cell phone question above—then it is generally safe to omit "don't know" as an option.

Multiple-Choice Questions. Multiple-choice questions are a popular option for many surveys because they are easy to answer and quick to analyze. Pay particular attention to response options to ensure that your list covers all possible answers. A question like "Do you use regular or premium gas in your car?" does not cover all possible answers. The question ignores the possibility of diesel or electric-powered cars. A better way of asking this question is given in Example 4.14.

Example 4.14

Which type(s) of fuel do you use in your primary vehicle?

O Regular gasoline

O Premium gasoline

O Diesel fuel

O Other [   ]

If you want only one answer from each person, be sure that the options are mutually exclusive. (See Example 4.15.)

Example 4.15

What is your current employment status?

O Employed full-time

O Employed part-time

O Unemployed

O Full-time student

This question does not take into account the fact that the respondent may be currently a student and employed part- or full-time. There are two solutions: Instruct respondents to "check all that apply," or rewrite the item as two questions. (See the following example.)

Example 4.16 a

What is your current employment status?

O Employed full-time

O Employed part-time

O Unemployed

Example 4.16 b

What is your current student status?

○ Full-time student

○ Part-time student

○ Not a student

Recent research evidence (Dillman, Smyth, Christian, & Stern, 2002; Smyth, Dillman, Christian, & Stern, 2006) indicates that forcing respondents to choose one answer from a list is preferable to the "check all that apply" format for Web surveys. In experimental studies, respondents took longer to answer forced-choice questions than check-all questions, suggesting a deeper level of processing of the response options.

Rankings. The online survey is one of the few venues in which ranking questions can be used effectively. To rank more than two or three items, it is important that respondents be able to view the complete list. The following is an example of using a matrix to present a ranking question.

Example 4.17

1. **Please rank what you look for in order of importance when selecting cleaning products, one is least important and five is most important. Each rank should be used only once.**

	1	2	3	4	5
Quality	○	○	○	○	○
Cost	○	○	○	○	○
Quantity	○	○	○	○	○
Brand name	○	○	○	○	○
Familiarity	○	○	○	○	○

Rating Scales. Selecting a scale for a survey question is not a trivial decision. Methodological research is equivocal when it comes to factors such as how many points and what kind of labels make the most effective scale questions. Nevertheless, we provide some general guidelines for writing scale questions:

> *Even or odd:* Even numbered scales tend to more effectively discriminate between the positive and negative positions as there is no neutral option. However, this can sometimes cause respondents who are genuinely neutral to hesitate and perhaps skip the question altogether. The use of this type of scale without a midpoint also has been shown to result in a positive skew in the data. The reasoning is that when forced to choose a side, most people opt to be "nice" and select the positive side

of the scale. If a respondent is truly neutral on a topic, then forcing him or her to any one side will yield invalid data and may alienate the participant.

Number of points: The number of points for your scale questions should be determined by how you intend to use the data. Although 10-point scales may seem to gather more data than 5-point scales, they do not necessarily discriminate more accurately among respondents. Also, in data analysis, these longer scales are typically collapsed into 3- or 5-point scales. The debate in the literature is ongoing; however, it is safe to say that 4- or 5-point scales will be serviceable for most attitude or opinion data collection.

Scale labels: Once the number of points on a scale has been decided, you'll next need to determine the labels for each scale point or, in some cases, whether or not you will use any labels. Some researchers prefer to anchor the end points, which means that only the first and last scale points are defined with words. Example 4.18 illustrates how an agreement scale can be set up.

Example 4.18

Strongly Disargree				Strongly Agree
○	○	○	○	○

Researchers using this approach argue that it prevents respondents from having to make decisions about the differences among word labels for each scale point. Though this may be true, it is also important that each respondent understand the meaning of each scale point. By labeling each scale point, respondents attach the same word or phrase to a particular place on the scale. This helps avoid respondent misinterpretation of scale definitions.

Example 4.19

Strongly Disargree	Disargree	Neutral	Agree	Strongly Agree
○	○	○	○	○

Whether you decide to define all of your scale points or only some, the labels attached can affect the validity of your results. Example 4.20 shows a typical product-rating question. The scale ranges from "excellent" to "poor." These words have connotative meanings for respondents—for example, they may associate the labels with grades in school. One individual may regard "good" as a high mark, whereas another might choose "good" to indicate an inadequate product, as in "it was only good." It is important to pretest questions on a small sample of your target population to ensure that respondents understand the scale labels (and the questions) the way you intended them to be understood.

Example 4.20: Product-Rating Scale

How would you rate this product?

    Excellent   Good   Fair   Poor

Contingency Questions

It is often necessary to ask one question in order to determine if the respondent is qualified to answer a subsequent question. This situation requires the use of contingency questions. For instance, in election polling, it would be useful to first ask if a respondent is a U.S. citizen before asking if he or she is registered to vote. A set of contingency questions might include the following.

Example 4.21

Are you a U.S. citizen?	Yes	No
Are you registered to vote?	Yes	No
Are you planning to vote in Tuesday's election?	Yes	No

This branching could continue further by asking respondents who said "yes" if they had decided on a candidate, who the candidate is, why they have chosen this candidate, and so on. Contingency questions are usually discouraged in paper-and-pencil self-administered questionnaires because respondents tend to become confused by having to skip questions and often follow the wrong branch of the question. When this happens, the researcher is forced to discard the data from that respondent as they do not follow a logical pattern. Online questionnaires, however, can be programmed to activate a different set of follow-up questions based on the options selected in previous questions. In other words, the respondents who click "no," indicating that they are not registered to vote, would not see the pages asking about voting intention and candidate choice.

Level of Measurement

There are four levels of measurement to consider when writing questions for your survey. To decide which is the most suitable, you will need to evaluate your data analysis and reporting needs (i.e., the level of statistical analysis required) as well as the appropriateness of the topic to the proposed level of measurement.

Nominal Data

The values associated with nominal variables fall into unordered categories—for example, ethnicity, eye color, or occupation. The response options for the ethnicity question—White, Hispanic, African American, Asian, and so on—are not associated with any numerical values and are not ordered in any way. Numbers may be associated with nominal response options, but it is important to realize that the numbers are arbitrary, that is, they do not have any inherent meaning. For example, we might assign the number 1 to blue, 2 to green, 3 to orange, 4 to yellow, and 5 to red. We might just as well label yellow 7, red 8, and so on.

Ordinal Data

Ordinal data can be rank ordered—for example, the outcome of a race: first place, second place, third place, and so on. There is reasoning behind the numbers: They tell us the order in which the contestants finished. However, the distances between the attributes are not equal; the winner may have finished 2 minutes ahead of the second-place contestant, who might have finished only 2 seconds ahead of the person in third place. On a survey, we might code education as follows: 1 = no high school degree, 2 = high school degree, 3 = some college, 4 = college degree, 5 = postgraduate education. Higher numbers mean more education. Rating scales are a frequently used form of ordinal measurement in survey research.

Interval Data

The numerical values associated with interval data provide an indication of relative position, and the distances between the values are interpretable. Age is an interval variable. If you have one 20-year-old respondent and one 40-year-old respondent, not only do you know that Respondent 2 is older than Respondent 1, you also know that Respondent 2 is twice as old as Respondent 1.

Ratio Data

Ratio measures have all the features of interval measures plus a zero that is meaningful. Weights, the number of customers, and the amount of money spent on an item are examples of variables that can be studied using ratio measurement.

The levels of measurement are hierarchical—that is, the current level includes all the qualities of the one below it plus a new element. Nominal data represent the most basic level of measurement, discriminating only among categories of responses. Ordinal data introduce the ability to rank responses. Interval measures provide meaningful distances between the values, and ratio measures add an absolute zero.

The decisions surrounding level of measurement should be made in light of the data analysis plan. Consider the income question. You might initially collect this information at the ratio level by asking respondents to record their annual income in an open-ended question providing a high degree of detail that allows for the greatest discrimination among respondents. If necessary, you could later recode the responses into the following ordinal categories: upper, middle, and low. If that was still more detail than you actually needed, you could further recode the answers to reflect the following nominal categories: income/no income. To provide the greatest options in data analysis, you should always collect data at the highest level of measurement possible because while you can make a ratio variable nominal, you cannot do the opposite.

Demographic Questions

Demographic questions ask for background information about respondents such as age, gender, education level, and income. The data are typically used to describe the respondents and sometimes to compare the characteristics of the sample with known population characteristics—from census data, for example. Demographic data also are used to segment and compare groups within the sample.

Much of what we have said up to this point can be applied to the writing of demographic questions; however, we devote a separate section to them for two reasons: (1) they are ubiquitous on survey questionnaires and (2) many people consider these items to be sensitive in nature, and unless they are carefully written, respondents may refuse to answer them. The basic questions are as follows:

1. Are you male or female?

2. What is your age?

3. What is the highest level of education you have completed?

4. What is your own yearly income?

5. What is your total household income, including all earners in your household?

6. What is your current marital status?

7. What is your religious affiliation?

8. What is your race or ethnicity?

9. What is the highest level of education your mother has completed?

10. What is the highest level of education your father has completed?

11. Are you employed outside the home?

12. How many hours per week do you work outside the home?

13. What is your occupation?

The number and form of the demographic questions used on a questionnaire will vary according to the survey objectives and the researcher's discipline. For many purposes, asking about religious affiliation will suffice; however, some researchers may find that this question by itself is not helpful and will choose to follow it with a question about degree of religiosity. Similarly, we use the categories of "male" and "female" as response options for the question of gender. Researchers occupied with more precise distinctions between biological differences and social categories may want to ask two questions: one addressing sex (male or female) and the other aimed at assessing gender (femininity and masculinity). As a general rule, ask only the demographic questions that are relevant to your survey objectives. Asking personal questions that seem unrelated to the rest of the questionnaire may make respondents suspicious and likely to abandon the survey. Furthermore, you will be needlessly lengthening your survey.

Place the demographic items near the end of the questionnaire and include a preface or introduction to the section—something like "We'd now like to gather some personal information about you. Remember, all of your answers are confidential." An exception to this is if a demographic question, like gender, is to be used as a filter question at the beginning of the survey.

Consider using closed-ended questions with ranges as response options for age and income. While it is always useful to collect precise data by leaving these questions open-ended, this benefit must be balanced by the sensitive nature of the questions. Many respondents feel uncomfortable typing in an exact number for their age or income, whereas checking a box provides the relative safety of being included in a category. Unless you absolutely need to know someone's exact age or income, provide the response options as follows.

Example 4.22 a

What is your age?

☐ 18–24

☐ 25–44

☐ 45–64

☐ 65 or older

Example 4.22 b

What is your annual income?

☐ Less than $10,000

☐ $10,000 to $19,999

☐ $20,000 to $29,999

☐ $30,000 to $39,999

☐ $40,000 to $49,999

☐ $50,000 to $59,999

☐ $60,000 to $69,999

☐ $70,000 or more

If you do need to know respondents' specific age, ask for date of birth. Most people are accustomed to including their date of birth on forms and are less anxious about it than typing in their age.

When considering the range of variation of the response options, it is necessary to know something about the sample. Are you surveying computer programmers, college students, or members of a professional association? For each sample, the ranges of age and income will differ. In addition to adhering to the basic rules of providing an exhaustive and mutually exclusive list of answer choices, think about whether the categories will adequately discriminate among respondents. For example, if you questioned corporate attorneys using the income measure above, you're likely to have most or all of the sample choosing the $70,000 or more category. While the data would be valid, they would not be particularly useful.

Questions about ethnicity and religion tend to be especially sensitive. You might need several screens to provide a truly exhaustive list of the categories.

One option is to use standardized categories. Useful examples of standard demographic items can be found at the National Opinion Research Center (www.norc.uchicago.edu/index.asp), the Center for Political Studies (www.isr .umich.edu/cps/), and the U.S. Census Bureau (www.census.gov). We also have included a list of standard demographic questions and answer options in Appendix C. An alternative is to leave questions about ethnicity and religion open-ended. Of course, you might get a wide range of answers and will need to spend time tabulating and possibly recoding the responses.

Guidelines for Asking Survey Questions

1. *Provide instructions:* Let the respondent know what to do on any particular question. The instruction should be simple—for example, "Select one option," "Select all that apply," "Rank the following options: 5 is the most prestigious, 1 is the least."

2. *Use everyday language:* Avoid jargon, slang, and abbreviations unless your sample is narrowly defined and you're certain that the language will be understood by the respondents. If it is necessary to use technical language that respondents may be unfamiliar with, include a hyperlink to the definition of the word.

3. *Write in complete sentences:* Instead of asking, "Age," ask "What is your age?"

4. *Write short, simple questions:* Long questions increase the risk of item nonresponse. A respondent is more likely to skip a question than to read it more than once for clarification. An exception to this rule is if you include a preface to a question to account for social desirability bias.

5. *Ask one question at a time:* Asking more than one question at a time renders data impossible to analyze. Consider this question: "Do you favor increased spending on sports and music programs?" A "yes" response may mean that the respondent favors more spending on sports, more spending on music, or both.

6. *Be consistent with your use of response options:* Constantly switching scales requires more space devoted to instructions and will lengthen the completion time of the survey.

7. *Use consistent wording and phrases throughout the questionnaire:* Questions can be set up with a lead phrase—for example, "How satisfied are you that our staff is . . . [knowledgeable] [responsive] [efficient], etc.?"

8. *Be sure that response options are meaningful to the respondents:* This is an issue of range—meaning that you make sure that the response options cover all possibilities for your respondents—and appropriateness of the question to the respondents, ensuring that the topics you're asking about are relevant to the target respondents.

(Continued)

(Continued)

9. *When comparing products don't label them "A" and "B":* This brings to mind grades, and respondents are likely to favor the "A" product over the one labeled "B." Use neutral labels, such as "M" and "N."

10. *Watch out for leading questions:* **Leading questions** are those that lead respondents to an answer. Consider this question: "The AIDS epidemic is a national emergency. It has already claimed more than 200,000 lives in the United States alone. Over one and a half million Americans now carry the AIDS virus. Do you favor increased federal spending on AIDS research programs?" The question could be corrected by eliminating the first three sentences.

Pretesting

Even the most well-crafted questions and carefully constructed response options sometimes fail to collect valid and reliable information. No textbook can cover all the ways respondents may misinterpret your questions. The only way to find out if your questions will work is to pretest your questionnaire.

To do this, you will need to select a small sample of your target population to complete the questionnaire and provide feedback about the questions and about the proper functioning of the technical elements of the survey. These individuals will not be able to participate in the actual survey, because they have been exposed to the questions. If your population is small and you are reluctant to conduct a pretest for fear of sacrificing potential respondents, consider looking for an analogous population and select pretest participants from that group. Do not, however, use your fellow researchers as pretest respondents; they may not catch jargon or leading questions, because they are familiar with the survey topic.

Pretesting is an extra step in the survey process and takes away from one of the benefits of online surveys—namely, speed. However, consider this: If you choose not to conduct a pretest and later find that the majority of your respondents skipped key questions because they didn't understand them or because the response options were inadequate, you will have to start over. Not only will this delay you, but you will have an additional problem: You will not be able to survey the same respondents about the same topic.

Summary

Valid questions are the lifeblood of surveys. We have covered some of the common question types, choices of response options, and levels of measurement; offered some suggestions for writing effective questions; and ended with a note on the importance of pretesting survey questions. We now turn our attention to constructing questionnaires.

5

Designing and Developing the Survey Instrument

O bservations of people who try to complete Web surveys suggest that two sources of significant frustration are lack of computer knowledge and poor questionnaire design (Dillman & Bowker, 2001). This often leads to premature termination of the survey. This finding as well as other research illustrate the need for thoughtful consideration regarding the design of online surveys. Online surveys have more flexibility in how they look, the response options, and the types of media that can be used than mail surveys; therefore, their design has unique considerations.

In this chapter, we examine survey design techniques in terms of appearance, readability, user friendliness, and technical compatibility. Topics such as color, font type and size, formats for response options, navigational guides, and **download** time are addressed. We also offer suggestions for making the questionnaire appropriate for your sample and accessible to people with dyslexia and visual impairments.

Questionnaire Design

The best survey questionnaires look professional and motivating, are easy to comprehend, are inviting and not intimidating, make answering the questions a clear and simple process, and are accessible to everyone in the target population. Many of the design principles applicable to self-administered paper questionnaires can be effectively applied to Web-based questionnaires. For example, the first question should be easy to answer, requiring no more than a few seconds of respondents' time; the questions should progress in a logical fashion; questions relating to the same topic should be kept together; and bolding or italicizing can be used to direct participants' attention to important words. In addition to these basic principles of good design, there are a number of important factors for Web survey designers to evaluate when constructing an online questionnaire. For example, Web surveys offer the opportunity to use a variety of exciting bells and whistles, including the ability to embed colorful images, video, and audio to enhance question-naires. When it comes to designing Web-based questionnaires, however, sim-plicity is usually best.

Design Principles for Web-Based Questionnaires

Dillman (2000) identified a set of design principles that can be applied to Web-based questionnaires. These principles were an extension of the earlier work of Dillman, Tortora, and Bowker (1998). The principles were devel-oped to account for the task of responding to online surveys, the computer resources required by the finished questionnaires, and the need to ensure compatibility across different computer platforms and **operating systems.** The following discussion is based on Dillman's design principles but modi-fied to reflect recent developments in online survey software and the increas-ing familiarity with online surveys in the population.

Welcome Screen

Introduce the Web questionnaire with a welcome screen that is motiva-tional, emphasizes the ease of responding, and instructs respondents on the action needed for proceeding to the next page. This will be the first screen the respondent sees (unless there is a language selection screen) when he or she clicks on the link to the survey. The welcome screen provides an oppor-tunity to describe or reiterate the purpose of the survey, explain how the respondent was selected for participation, discuss the conditions of anonymity and confidentiality, and explain how to collect or redeem incen-tives if applicable. Welcome screens are best when kept brief and are most appropriate for longer questionnaires. If the questionnaire is only one or two screens long, the welcome message could be included at the top of the first screen. (See Figure 5.1 for an example of a welcome screen.)

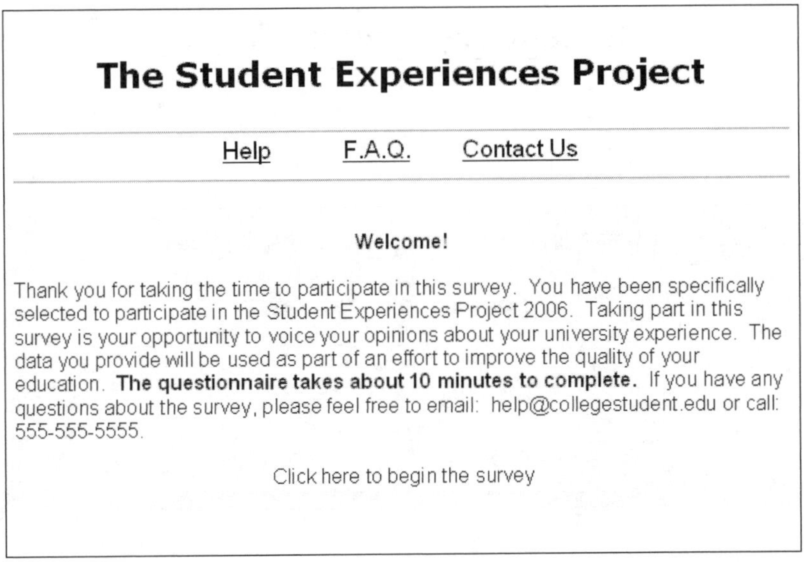

The Student Experiences Project

Help   F.A.Q.   Contact Us

Welcome!

Thank you for taking the time to participate in this survey. You have been specifically selected to participate in the Student Experiences Project 2006. Taking part in this survey is your opportunity to voice your opinions about your university experience. The data you provide will be used as part of an effort to improve the quality of your education. **The questionnaire takes about 10 minutes to complete.** If you have any questions about the survey, please feel free to email: help@collegestudent.edu or call: 555-555-5555.

Click here to begin the survey

Figure 5.1   Welcome Page Example

Access Control

Provide a personal identification number (PIN) number for limiting access to people in the sample. PIN codes (or passwords) are primarily necessary when working with probability samples from closed populations. When attempting to generalize survey results to populations, it is important that only those respondents selected for the sample complete the questionnaire; uninvited participants may or may not meet your inclusion criteria and could substantially distort the survey results. Passwords can be included on the survey invitation, and the space in which to enter the password should appear on the questionnaire welcome screen. The password should be kept simple and not too lengthy. Figure 5.2 is an example of a password field that may be included on a welcome page. (*Note:* It is generally not necessary to password protect questionnaires using nonprobability samples from open populations.)

First Question

As respondents work their way through questionnaires, they become more and more invested in the process and are less likely to abandon the survey.

Student Experiences Survey

Please enter your password in the field below

For example: aaa.aaa

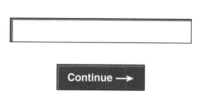

Figure 5.2   Password Protecting the Questionnaire

It stands to reason, then, that abandonment is most likely to occur early in the questionnaire. It is therefore essential that the first question be short, simple, and, if possible, fun for respondents. The first question sets the tone for the rest of the questionnaire; if it is lengthy or complicated or presents unfamiliar response scales, respondents may infer that this is indicative of all the questionnaire items and decide not to complete the survey. For these reasons, it is best to restrict first questions to closed-ended items that present radio buttons or check boxes for responses. Figure 5.3 shows two examples of first questions. Note that the first example requires respondents to indicate their satisfaction level and then rank each option; the second example requires one task and is presented in a familiar format.

Conventional Format

Present each question in a conventional format similar to that normally used on self-administered paper questionnaires. Respondents may or may not be familiar with Web questionnaires, but it is likely that if you are

1.	Please indicate your satisfaction. Then rank the importance from 1 to 5.				
		Satisfaction			Importance Ranking
		Dissatisfied	Neutral	Satisfied	
	Software-R-Us as a place to work	○	○	○	☐
	The company's training program	○	○	○	☐
	Your compensation at Software-R-Us	○	○	○	☐
	The company's equity structure	○	○	○	☐
	Your health care benefits at Software-R-Us	○	○	○	☐

(a) Poor first question: requires ranking and rating of five items.

1. How satisfied are you with the training you received from your supervisor?

Completely satisfied	Somewhat satisfied	Neither satisfied nor dissatisfied	Somewhat dissatisfied	Completely dissatisfied
○	○	○	○	○

(b) Better first question: one question with a standard response scale.

Figure 5.3   Examples of First Questions From a New Employee Survey

surveying adults, they will be familiar with paper questionnaires. Following the rules of good questionnaire design developed for paper questionnaires within the context of the Web survey will foster familiarity with the instrument and thus increase respondents' ability to complete the questionnaire quickly and accurately. Specifically, conventional **formatting** includes numbering questions, left justifying text, and presenting response options either to the right of or directly below the questions to which they refer.

Color

Color can easily be added to online surveys without additional cost, and it can enhance the appearance of the survey, assist with navigation, and motivate the respondent; however, color should be used cautiously. The use of color should be restricted so that figure/ground consistency and readability are maintained, navigational flow is unimpeded, and measurement properties of questions are maintained. Also, colors do not necessarily have the same appearance on different computer screens, so for most purposes, it is safest to use the standard 256-color palette.

Colors generally have feelings and meanings associated with them. Table 5.1 lists some examples of common color associations for adults in the United States.

Table 5.1   Color Associations for Adults in the United States

Color	Positive Associations	Negative Associations
Red	Power, love, fire, passion, intimacy, courage	Danger, aggression, blood, hot, stop
Green	Money, freshness, envy, nature, growth	Inexperience, misfortune
Purple	Royalty, luxury	
Pink	Female, cute, soft, gentle	
Blue	Male, sky, water, peace, truth, calm	Sadness, depression
Orange	Autumn, Halloween, creativity	Caution
Yellow	Happiness, sunshine, optimism, summer	Illness, hazard
Brown	Earth, nature	Bland
Gray	Maturity, dignity	Gloomy, conservative, boring
White	Winter, virginity, clean, innocent, truth, peace, snow	Cold, sterility, clinical
Black	Formality, style, power, depth	Death, evil, mourning, night, mystery, fear

Colors do not necessarily have the same meanings on an international level. For example, death and mourning are represented by white in Asia, yellow in the Philippines, and black in the United States. Be conscious of these differences in the meaning of color when you have an international response pool.

Combining Colors. Many survey software programs offer developers choices of color palettes that combine two or more colors for individual questionnaires. These combinations are often given labels such as "desert sunset," "midnight ocean," and "orange sherbet," with the resulting design faintly resembling how one might imagine these scenes to be colored. It is tempting to experiment with these options; however, it is important to consider readability and mood when combining colors.

Readability. For maximum readability, there should be high contrast between the text color and the background color. Dark text on a light background is easy to read. It goes without saying that dark text on a dark background or light text on a light background is difficult to read. Light text on a dark background is also easy to read, but it should be used sparingly as it can be tiring to the eyes to read large amounts of text on a dark background. Below are some additional guidelines for using colors:

- Bright colors are easier to see than pastels.
- Using too many colors can create a confused and cluttered effect.
- Multi colors are useful for many charts, graphs, maps, and so on.
- Some people experience color insensitivity. The most common is reduced sensitivity to reds and greens; about 10% of men experience this "color blindness." If you put red letters on a green background, 10% of the men in your audience will not be able to read your questionnaire.

Mood. Colors used in combination can create different moods and feelings compared with colors used alone. Basic color theory indicates that the following color combinations are harmonious:

- Two colors opposite of each other on the color wheel
- Any three colors equally spaced around the color wheel forming a triangle
- Any four colors forming a rectangle, each opposite of each other on the color wheel (see the 12-part color wheel in Figure 5.4)

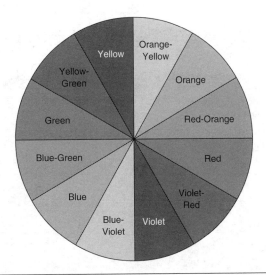

Figure 5.4   Twelve-Part Color Wheel

(For information on color and vision deficits, please see the section titled Making Your Survey Accessible to Everyone, later in this chapter.)

Technological Issues Related to Appearance

Be attentive to differences in the visual appearance of questionnaires that result from different browsers, operating systems, screen configurations, partial screen displays, and wrap-around text.

Nonresponse to a survey can occur because of incompatibilities with hardware or software. What the developer sees on his or her screen is not necessarily what another viewer sees. It is important to test the survey using different browsers—that is, Internet Explorer, Netscape, and Firefox—as well as different operating systems—that is, Windows XP, Windows 2000, Mac OS, and so on.

Consider the physical placement and presentation of items when reviewing questionnaires on different computers. Problems with physical distance between points on response scales were noted by Dillman and Bowker (2001) when screen resolution configurations changed from 800×600 to another configuration—that is, 640×480 or 1024×768. These numbers represent the number of **pixels** that make up the vertical and horizontal dimensions on a computer screen and affect the appearance of text and images. Pixels per inch (ppi) is a measure of sharpness on a screen; in general, the more pixels there are, the sharper the screen image will be. (Figure 5.5 shows how the same questionnaire looks vastly different depending on the

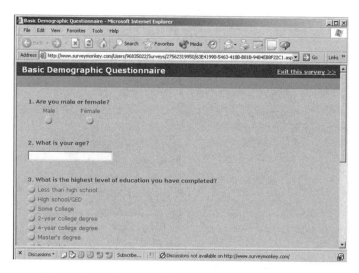

(a) Demographic questionnaire using 800×600 screen display

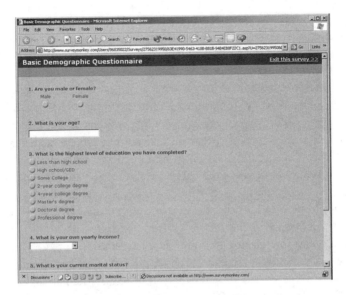

(b) Demographic questionnaire using 1,024 × 768 screen display

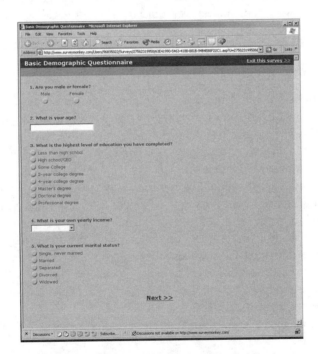

(c) Demographic questionnaire using 1,280 × 1,024 screen display

Figure 5.5   Questionnaire Display With Different Screen Configurations

screen configuration.) According to www.WebUsability.com, the most common monitor setting is 1024 × 768 pixels or higher (60% of Web users), 800 × 600 is the second most common setting, and less than 1% of Web users have their monitors set to 640 × 480.

There are two schools of thought when it comes to creating Web content, including online surveys, for different screen settings. The first advocates building surveys that can be easily viewed by the greatest number of individuals in your sample; currently, that means creating surveys with the 1024 × 768 or higher screen configuration in mind. The second school of thought suggests developing surveys that can be viewed accurately by *all* potential respondents; that is, if any users still have their screens set to 640 × 480, the survey should be created with this fact in mind. Critics of this second position claim that you will end up with a questionnaire that looks amateurish on most screens, in order to accommodate less than 1% of Web users.

Computer technology and the way people use it is changing faster than we can write these words; in addition to testing questionnaires on a variety of computers, online survey researchers will need to investigate the current state of Web usability and evaluate those conditions in light of their particular target populations and survey objectives when deciding on the most appropriate way to display Web questionnaires.

Instructions

Instructions for completing the questionnaire should always be included, no matter how obvious the procedure may seem. When writing directions, avoid jargon and do not use abbreviations without writing out the words first.[1] A link to a glossary of abbreviations and terms can be beneficial if you have doubts about respondents' familiarity with the terms. Directions need not be lengthy, but they should be comprehensive, especially for people who are unfamiliar with online surveys (see Figure 5.6). Consider writing brief directions and including a link to more detailed directions for people who may need them. It is best to place the links for the directions for answering specific questions next to the question instead of placing them all at the beginning of the survey and overwhelming the reader. For example, the first question that uses radio buttons may have a link that explains how to answer the question or change answers.

Instructions might address some or all of the following questions:

- Does the respondent have to answer all the questions?
- Can the respondent select only one answer for the question or more than one?
- How does the respondent move to the next question?

- Is there a time limit for completing the questionnaire?
- Can the respondent skip a question and return to it later?
- How does the respondent change an answer?
- Does the respondent need to single or double click on the answer?
- Can the respondent begin the survey and return to it later?
- If the respondent returns to complete the survey later, will he or she have to start all over again?

Online Survey Instructions

- The survey is very simple to complete and should only take about 10 minutes or less of your time.
- If you are unsure about a specific service provided by your organization, you may choose to skip that question and complete it after you have obtained the information needed (re-clicking the link at a later time will return you automatically to uncompleted items, or you may also click the "back" key anytime while taking the survey).
- Only one response per individual please.
- You may move back to a previous page and revise your responses at any time. When all answers are completed, simply click the "submit" tab and you will be asked to select your gift of appreciation. **The first 50 respondents are eligible to receive NIKE running/walking shoes!**
- **All surveys should be completed by July 14, 2006!**
- Should you wish to complete the survey by hand we will be happy to mail a hard copy to you.
- Please contact us at 555-555-5555 if you need assistance. Remember: all surveys should be completed by July 14, 2006!
- Thank you for your participation.

Click here to begin the survey

Figure 5.6   Survey Instructions

For people who want to participate in the survey but prefer not to complete an online questionnaire or are unable to do so, it is important to provide information about alternative ways to participate—for example, by sending a paper version of the questionnaire via postal mail. Of course, if alternative modes of participation are allowed, it is necessary to configure the alternative questionnaires so that they resemble the online versions as closely as possible.

Formats for Response Options

When creating online surveys, the developer has a choice of several ways to present the response options, including radio buttons, check boxes, drop-down menus, rank order matrices, constant sum, and open-ended text boxes. Regardless of the combination of response options you select, it is important to maintain consistency in terms of font type and size, width of response categories, and colors used throughout the questionnaire. Varying any of these elements may cause respondents to interpret some questions as being more important than others.

Radio Buttons. A radio button is a small circle with text next to it; when the respondent clicks on the circle, it is filled in with a smaller, solid circle or sometimes with a check mark (see Figure 5.7). Radio buttons are traditionally

9. How often do you shop in the Lakeview District?

⊃ Daily
⊃ About once a week
⊃ About once a month
⊃ Rarely
⊃ Never

(a) Multiple choice

10. Do you agree or disagree with the following statements about the store you visited?

	Strongly Agree	Agree	Disagree	Strongly Disagree	N/A
The store was conveniently located.	✓	⊃	⊃	⊃	⊃
The store hours were convenient for my shopping needs.	⊃	✓	⊃	⊃	⊃
The store had a good selection of products.	⊃	✓	⊃	⊃	⊃
The merchandise displays were attractive.	⊃	✓	⊃	⊃	⊃
The merchandise I wanted was in stock.	⊃	⊃	⊃	⊃	✓

(b) Likert-type scale

10. Using a 1 to 10 point scale where 1 means "not at all important" and 10 means "very important" how important are the following items to you when choosing a president? The candidate's ...

	1	2	3	4	5	6	7	8	9	10
positions on issues	⊃	⊃	⊃	⊃	⊃	⊃	⊃	⊃	⊃	⊃
age	⊃	⊃	⊃	⊃	⊃	⊃	⊃	⊃	⊃	⊃
education	⊃	⊃	⊃	⊃	⊃	⊃	⊃	⊃	⊃	⊃
political party	⊃	⊃	⊃	⊃	⊃	⊃	⊃	⊃	⊃	⊃
honesty	⊃	⊃	⊃	⊃	⊃	⊃	⊃	⊃	⊃	⊃
religion	⊃	⊃	⊃	⊃	⊃	⊃	⊃	⊃	⊃	⊃
spouse	⊃	⊃	⊃	⊃	⊃	⊃	⊃	⊃	⊃	⊃
military experience	⊃	⊃	⊃	⊃	⊃	⊃	⊃	⊃	⊃	⊃

(c) One to 10-point rating scale

Figure 5.7   Radio Button Examples

used when the respondent must select exactly one choice from a list—that is, clicking on a nonselected button will deselect whichever other button was previously selected. Radio buttons are useful for multiple-choice, Likert-type scale, and other scale questions. Generally, the response options for multiple-choice questions are listed vertically, while the options for rating scale questions are displayed horizontally, either next to the item or directly below it.

Check Boxes. A check box is a small box with text next to it. As the name implies, clicking on check boxes places a check mark in the selected box. They are most often used when respondents are permitted to select more than one option from a list, such as in the "select all that apply" type of question (see Figure 5.8). Check box responses, like radio button responses, can be programmed to accept only one response from a list if the researcher wishes.

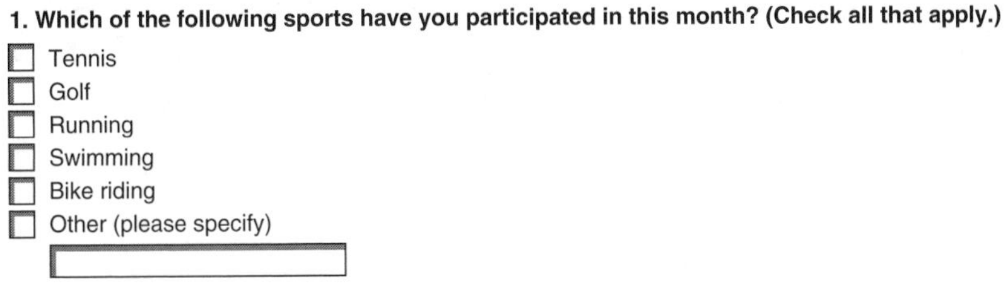

1. Which of the following sports have you participated in this month? (Check all that apply.)

☐ Tennis
☐ Golf
☐ Running
☐ Swimming
☐ Bike riding
☐ Other (please specify)
    [_____]

Figure 5.8   Check Box Example

Drop-Down Menus. A drop-down menu has a title that is visible, but the contents (response choices) are shown only when the respondent clicks the title or a small arrow next to the title. The participant selects from the list by dragging the mouse from the menu title to the response option and releasing or by clicking the title and then clicking the response choice (see Figure 5.9). If possible, and practical, it best to avoid using response categories in which the respondent cannot see all the options. Users may not be aware of how to use them or might not want to take the extra step to scroll down to see all the choices. One common problem among inexperienced Web users occurs when a default answer appears in the visible window of a drop-down menu (as in the first example in Figure 5.9). The respondent sees that the window is filled in and believes that he has already answered the question; or he may not realize that clicking on the arrow will provide more choices.

That being said, drop-down menus are effective when the list of response options is lengthy and would result in excessive scrolling on the page to see all the options and to get to the next question. It is important not to overuse drop-down menus—for example, for questions that have a few response

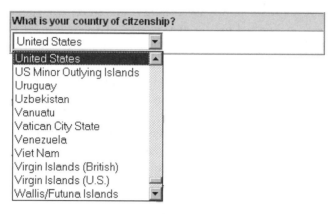

(a) Drop-down menu with a default option appearing in the visible text box

In which state do you live?   - Select One -   ▼

(b) Drop-down menu with an instruction appearing in the visible text box

Figure 5.9   Drop-Down Menu Examples

options that can easily be displayed beneath or next to the question. Moreover, when drop-down menus are being used, the visible window should not be left blank or be filled in with a default option; instead, include a "click here" or "select one" instruction.

Rank-Order Matrices. A rank-order matrix allows respondents to rank a list of options in order of preference or importance (see Figure 5.10). Respondents are not permitted to give the same rank to more than one option, and all options must be ranked before the respondent is allowed to move on to the next question. Online surveys are a good venue for this type of question, because they will not accept the problematic answers that

2. Please rank the following sources of information in your department.
Place a "1" next to the source you prefer the most, a "2" next to the
source you prefer second most, and so on. No two sources can have the same rank.

[ ] Immediate supervisor
[ ] Company newsletter
[ ] Coworkers
[ ] E-mail distribution lists
[ ] Bulletin boards

Figure 5.10   Rank Order

sometimes appear on paper questionnaires, such as respondents reporting that all options are equally important by writing in a "1" next to every item on a list. However, they do require effort on the respondent's part, and being forced to rank all items (or seeing error messages when trying to assign the same rank to two items) can cause frustration. To simplify the task, it is best to limit the number of items to be ranked to five or fewer.

Constant Sum. A constant sum question asks respondents to assign values or percentages across options so that the total sums to a predetermined amount. For example, you might want to know the percentage of an employee's workday spent on a variety of tasks, such as inventory control, customer service, and correspondence. The same question could be asked in terms of number of hours per day, assuming that an employee works an 8-hour day.

Like the ranking question, constant sum requires a good deal of effort on the part of the respondent as he or she must consider each of the response options relative to the others and to the total. The potential for error is higher in constant sum than in other types of questions—for example, typing in a set of values that sum to more than 100% will activate an error message. Likewise, leaving empty boxes will result in error messages (a zero must be entered for activities in which the respondent is not engaged). The likely result of being faced with a series of error messages is abandonment of the survey. When considering using constant sum questions, evaluate the cognitive and technical difficulty of the task you are asking respondents to perform to ensure that it is appropriate for your target population. (See Figure 5.11 for an example of a constant sum question.)

2. Please indicate the percentage of your workday you spend on the following activities. (The total must add up to 100%)

	Reading e-mail
	Answering the phone
	Taking orders
	Resolving customer complaints
	Developing new projects
	Other

Figure 5.11   Constant Sum

Open-Ended Text Boxes. Open-ended text boxes allow respondents to type in free text. The sizes of text boxes vary widely; options include short boxes that require one-word answers, single-line boxes for short phrases or sentences, and long boxes for detailed answers or comments. The length of respondents' answers will be guided by the amount of space they have to write in. Of course, this doesn't mean that respondents will necessarily fill long comment boxes with text or even respond to them at all. However, if you're looking for short answers, providing a one-word or single-line box is a way to prevent respondents from expounding on their answers. Figure 5.12 is an example of an open-ended text box.

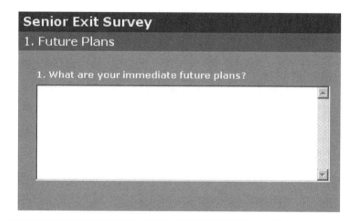

Figure 5.12   Open-Ended Text Box

Requiring Answers

It is best not to require respondents to provide an answer to each question before being allowed to answer any subsequent ones. Requiring answers to questions that may be difficult, embarrassing, or not applicable is frustrating to respondents and poses ethical issues. The ethical norm of voluntary participation applies to the survey as a whole and any part of it. In no other survey mode are respondents forced to answer particular questions. In interview questionnaires, respondents can refuse to answer any question and still continue with the survey; in paper questionnaires, they can simply leave questions unmarked. If you find it necessary to have answers to all questions, it is advisable to include the option of "don't know," "not applicable," or "decline to state" as possible choices.

One-Page Versus Multipage Questionnaires

In many situations, it will be at the discretion of the questionnaire developer whether to place all the survey items on one page or on multipages. Some decisions are obvious: If the entire questionnaire is three or four questions long, it is not necessary to use multipages; if the survey contains dozens of questions relating to a variety of topics, multipages are in order. Whenever skip logic is used, multipages are necessary. Figure 5.13 is an example of an "association membership questionnaire" where all the questions are on one page. The respondent scrolls from one question to the next and clicks the "submit" button when he or she is finished. It is a relatively simple procedure and closely resembles the process of completing a paper questionnaire, which may be useful if data from different survey modes are to be combined.

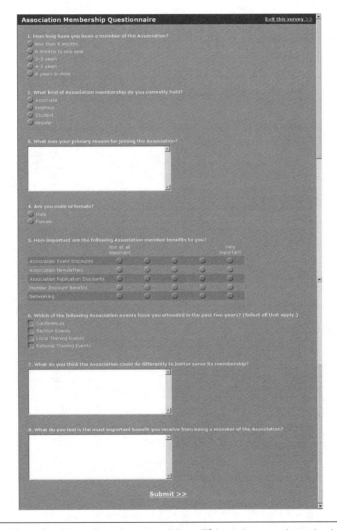

Figure 5.13   One-Page Questionnaire (*Note:* This entire questionnaire is contained on one Web page. Respondents scroll down the page to see all the questions.)

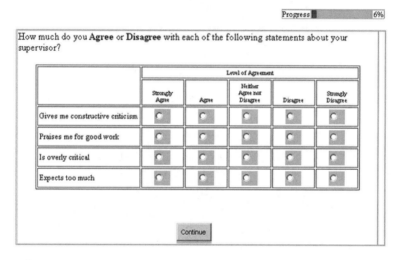

(a) Multipage questionnaire (Screen 1)

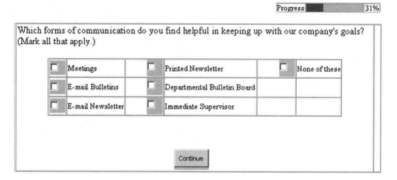

(b) Multipage questionnaire (Screen 2)

(c) Multipage questionnaire (Screen 3)

(d) Multipage questionnaire (Screen 4)

(e) Multipage questionnaire (Screen 5)

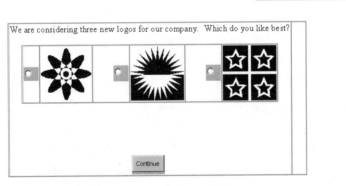

Thank you very much for completing our survey.

(f) Multipage questionnaire (Screen 6)

Figure 5.14   Multipage Questionnaire

It is possible to place each question on its own page (see Figure 5.14). Some researchers prefer this option because respondents focus on one question at a time, perhaps mitigating order effects. Order effects occur if respondents' answers to particular questions are influenced by previously recorded answers. The reasoning is that it is easier to scroll up on a single page than it is to hit the "back" button to review a previous answer.

The research evidence relating to respondent fatigue and premature termination of one-page versus multipage online surveys is ambiguous. Some of the evidence indicates that excessive scrolling is burdensome to respondents, while other research claims that too much clicking ("next," "back," etc.) is annoying. With the caveats regarding skip logic and possible order effects in mind, common sense suggests using one-page formats for short questionnaires and multipage formats for longer surveys, with questions grouped by topic or response format on the same pages.

Double and Triple Banking

When the number of answer choices exceeds the number that can be displayed on one screen, consider double (or triple) banking with appropriate navigational instructions added (see Figure 5.15). If the number of response

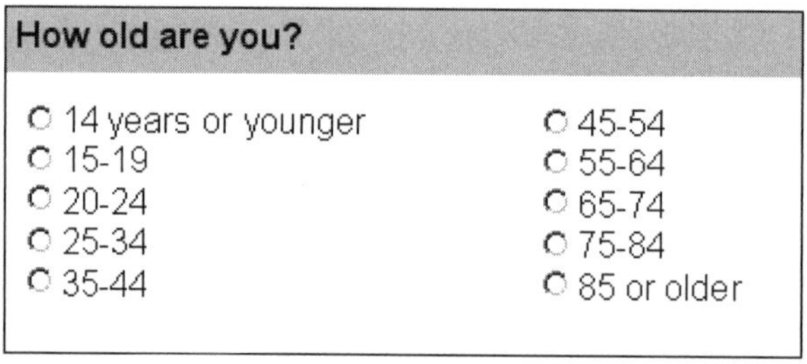

How old are you?

○ 14 years or younger	○ 45-54
○ 15-19	○ 55-64
○ 20-24	○ 65-74
○ 25-34	○ 75-84
○ 35-44	○ 85 or older

(a) Double banking with box enclosure

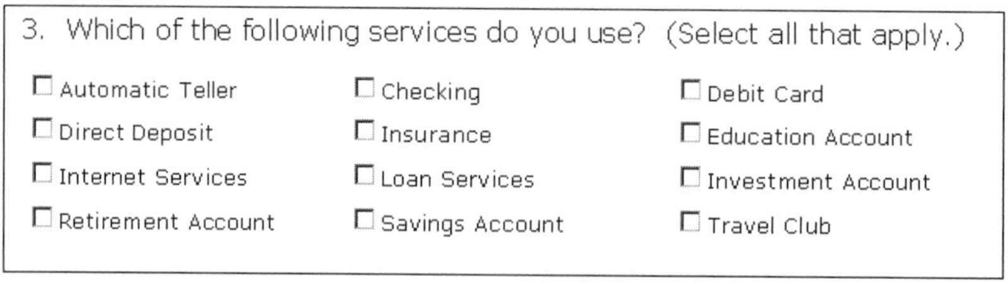

3. Which of the following services do you use? (Select all that apply.)

☐ Automatic Teller	☐ Checking	☐ Debit Card
☐ Direct Deposit	☐ Insurance	☐ Education Account
☐ Internet Services	☐ Loan Services	☐ Investment Account
☐ Retirement Account	☐ Savings Account	☐ Travel Club

(b) Triple banking with box enclosure

Figure 5.15   Double and Triple Banking

options exceeds what will fit in two or three columns on one screen, consider other options such as drop-down menus.

Navigation Guides

Getting lost when taking a survey is frustrating and can cause respondents to drop out before completing the survey. People taking the survey will have different levels of computer competency and comfort. Help respondents navigate through the survey within a short time and with limited frustration by providing clear directions and guideposts. Navigational guideposts assist the respondent in completing the survey without getting discouraged or lost. The guideposts are the road map of the survey.

As when looking at a road map, it is helpful for the reader to have an understanding of the location and how far he or she is from the destination point, which is the end of the survey. This can be done in different ways. One is to identify the screen number the respondent is currently on and the number of screens in total. For example, you could place screen numbers on each page, which would be similar to page numbers in a book—that is, screen 3 of 15. You also could identify the respondents' location by question number—for example, question 4 of 20. Another way is to identify the percentage of the survey that has been completed by using a progress bar (see Figure 5.16).

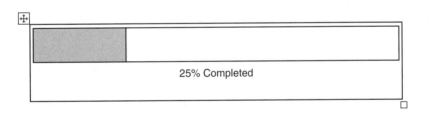

Figure 5.16   Progress Bar

Signs also should be posted on your road map. The signs will indicate to the respondent how to go back, move forward, and submit the survey. Road signs usually have a designated color or shape—that is, brown signs indicate a historic site, yellow signs indicate caution, and "yield" signs are triangular. The signs that you post on your survey road map also should have consistent colors and shapes and be placed in a consistent location on each screen of the questionnaire (see Figure 5.17).

5. Please answer the following questions in your own words.

- What most **attracts** you to this company?

- What most **irritates** you about this company?

....

Figure 5.17   Navigation Aids

Table 5.2   Examples of Serif and Sans Serif Fonts

Serif Fonts	Sans Serif Fonts
Times New Roman	Arial
Courier New	Verdana
Georgia	Comic Sans MS
Century Schoolbook	Century Gothic
Goudy Old Style	Tahoma
Monotype Corsiva	Bradley Hand ITC

Font Type and Text Size

There are two main types of fonts: serif and sans serif. Serif fonts, such as Times New Roman, Courier New, and Georgia, have small appendages on the top and bottom of the letters. The appendages help to distinguish each letter and make it easier to read strings of text (see Table 5.2). The sans serif fonts, such as Arial, Verdana, and Comic Sans MS, are simpler and are generally better for short phrases such as headings (Morrison & Noyes, 2003). The question of interest to Web survey designers is what font type is the easiest and fastest to read and what font size is the most effective. A number of studies have focused on fonts for online reading.

A study conduced by Bernard and Mills (2000) examined Times New Roman and Arial fonts for readability, reading time, perception of legibility and sharpness, and general preference. Thirty-five adult participants were asked to read passages with 10-point Arial, 12-point Arial, 10-point Times New Roman, and 12-point Times New Roman. The highlights of the study were as follows:

- No significant differences were found in detecting errors in the reading passage.
- Participants could read the passage fastest with 12-point Times New Roman (M = 365 seconds); the 10-point Arial font came second (M = 368 seconds).
- Participants reported on a 7-point scale that the 12-point Arial font (M = 5.7) and 12-point Times New Roman font (M = 5.6) were the most legible.
- Participants reported on a 7-point scale that the 12-point Arial font (M = 4.8) and the 12-point Times New Roman font (M = 4.7) were similar in their sharpness.
- The researchers determined that the mean preference choice between all font sizes, types, and formats was the 12-point Arial, followed by the 12-point Times New Roman font. The 12-point Arial was selected as the preferred choice approximately 33 times, and the 12-point Times New Roman was selected as the first choice approximately 27 times. Overall, there is a slight preference for the 12-point Arial font over the 12-point Times New Roman font for reading on the Web. The difference was not statistically significant.

In another study that assessed font types in terms of mood and the readers' general preference, similar results were found (Bernard, Mills, Peterson, & Storrer, 2001). Twenty-two adult participants were asked to read passages presented in the following 12-point fonts: Agency FB, Arial, Comic Sans MS, Tahoma, Verdana, Courier New, Georgia, Goudy Old Style, Century Schoolbook, Times New Roman, Bradley Hand ITC, and Monotype Corsiva.

The researchers first computed a reading score based on font legibility and its associated reading time. Participants were then asked to rate the fonts for readability and aesthetic appeal. No significant differences between font legibility were found. The top-rated three fonts in each of the categories and their scores can be found in Table 5.3. It is important to note that the differences between the top-rated fonts were minimal.

No significant differences were found in terms of legibility. Courier and Times were perceived as being the most businesslike, and Comic was perceived as being the most fun and youthful font. The two fonts Bradley and Corsiva were perceived as having the most personality and being the most elegant; they also were seen as being low in legibility and in businesslike appearance, and they obtained the lowest rating in font preference.

Bernard and Mills (2000) studied children's font preferences when reading online. Thirty-seven participants between 9 and 11 years of age were involved in a study that compared preferences of 12- and 14-point fonts. Four font types were evaluated: Arial, Times New Roman, Courier New, and Comic Sans MS. Children preferred the 14-point fonts as they were perceived as being easier and faster to read and more attractive. Comic Sans MS was the preferred choice in all three measures (easy to read, reading faster, and attractiveness), with Arial as the second choice. When surveying children, 14-point Comic Sans MS is the preferred choice.

Table 5.3   Top Three Fonts in Each Category

Reading Time	Perceived Legibility	Perceived as Being Businesslike	Perceived as Youthful and Fun	Font Preference
1. Tahoma (270 seconds)	1. Courier	1. Times New Roman	1. Comic	1. Arial
2. Times New Roman (273 seconds)	2. Comic and Verdana	2. Courier	2. Bradley	2. Verdana and Georgia
3. Verdana (280 seconds)	3. Times New Roman	3. Schoolbook	3. Verdana	3. Comic

SOURCE: Data based on Bernard, Mills, Peterson, and Storrer (2001).

If your target audience is older adults, you also should use a 14-point font but opt for something like Arial. Twenty-seven participants ranging from 62 to 83 years of age were tested by Bernard, Liao, and Mills (2001). Four fonts were assessed in the study: Times New Roman, Georgia, Arial, and Verdana. Twelve- and 14-point font sizes were used in the study. In terms of readability, the 14-point font size had significantly greater reading efficiency than the 12-point font. The 14-point font also had faster reading time and a greater perception of legibility. The preferred fonts were the 14-point Arial and Georgia.

In sum, the number of studies on font types and online reading is limited, and none have been conducted specifically focusing on online surveys. Overall, Arial and Times New Roman are similar in terms of legibility and preference, and 14-point fonts are preferred by children and older adults.

Images, Graphs, and Charts

Images, graphs, and charts should be used sparingly when creating online surveys. They can greatly increase the download time, and depending on your target audience, the respondents may not know how to interpret them. On the other hand, judicious use of images can provide a context for questionnaire items and potentially increase the validity of answers. Figure 5.18 shows the same question presented with two different photos. Without having to read extra text, respondents are given an important clue about the context of the question and immediately understand that in the first question they should include visits to fast food restaurants, whereas the second refers to fine dining.

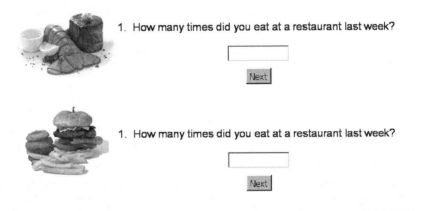

Figure 5.18   Questions With Images

Motion, Sound, and Links

Technology enables survey designers to add motion, sound, links, graphics, and **java applets**. All these features can make the survey more attractive, enticing, interesting, and entertaining, but these same features also can increase the time to download the survey and even make the potential respondent's computer crash. Such experiences can cause a lower response rate or frustration with the organization that hosts or disseminated the survey. While these high-tech features are compelling, the rule of thumb when it comes to online survey design is to keep it simple. To estimate the download time of your survey, you can use a download time calculator, which you can access at http://download.stormloader.com/.

Dillman, Tortora, Conrad, and Bowker (1998) found that surveys that download faster had a higher response rate than more elaborate ones that took longer to download. The researchers created a plain version and a fancy version of the same survey. The plain version required 317K of memory, and the required time for transmission on a 28.8 modem was at least 120 seconds. This version had no HTML tables or color. The fancy version required 959K of memory and took approximately 345 seconds for transmission. Of the people who logged on to the plain version, 93.1% completed the entire survey; 82.1% who logged on to the fancy version completed the questionnaire. The respondents of the plain survey completed an average of 166 questions. The respondents of the fancy survey completed an average of 156 questions.

Making Your Survey Accessible to Everyone

To reduce coverage bias as much as possible, it is important that online surveys are accessible to everyone in the target population. Ensuring that individuals with visual or learning disabilities or who speak a different language can complete the questionnaire is methodologically sound, ethically responsible, and sometimes legally required.

Language

If your target audience is an international one or includes people who may have limited English skills, you may want to consider translating your survey into languages other than English. Some software programs will allow the developer to convert a survey written in English into another language, while others such as Zoomerang will translate your survey and the responses into another language for a fee. Figure 5.19 shows how the Inquisite survey

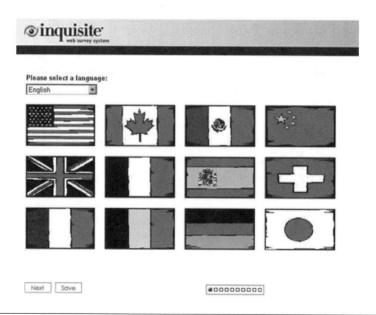

Figure 5.19   Language Selection Page

SOURCE: Reprinted with permission of Inquisite, Inc.

software system presents language options for respondents; this page should be the first one a respondent sees, before the welcome screen.

Visual Impairments

For people with visual disabilities, there are assistive software programs called screen readers. These screen readers enable the person to listen to the information on the Web page as the software reads the content of the Web page out loud. Some Web-based hosts, such as WebSurveyor, are accessible to people using screen readers.

When using screen readers, one factor that can contribute to poor Web access relates to graphic images. Screen readers read basic text, so graphics that do not contain an ALT tag will not be read. The ALT tag provides the reader with textual information about the graphic image. This is really essential if the graphic contains a link. If an ALT tag does not exist, then the person using the screen reader will not know that the information exists. It is not difficult to create an ALT tag. For example, if you have an image that displays the words "Log In," the HTML code may be as follows:

```
<IMG SRC="loginphoto.jpg" ALT="login">
```

When creating tables, organize the information from left to right instead of from top to bottom to help ensure greater understanding of the information (Academic Computing and Communications Center, n.d.).

To assist designers in creating accessible Web sites, the World Wide Web Consortium (W3C) created the Web Access Initiative guidelines. The W3C created 14 accessibility guidelines, which can be found at www.w3.org/TR/WCAG10/#Guidelines. You can test your page for accessibility in order to identify and resolve accessibility issues. The W3C has a Web site, www.cast.org/bobby, or you can use, www.usablenet.com.

Color deficits are another type of visual disability. About 8% of men and 0.5% of women have some form of color blindness (Newman, 2000). That could translate into 1 in 12 visitors for some Web sites. According to Newman, 99% of people who are color-blind have trouble distinguishing between red and green.

Bright and distinct colors are the easiest to distinguish. Using shades of a color can make it difficult to decipher. Exaggerate differences between foreground and background colors by using background colors that make the other image stand out—that is, red against white. Avoid colors of similar lightness near each other. Use more than one color to design your Web survey. If a link is in blue, then the reader may not be able to determine that it is a link.

Therefore, it is a good idea to make the link a different color and underline it as well.

Learning Disabilities

Dyslexia is a reading disability that affects almost 10% of the United States population (Able Access Net, 1999). As many as 80% of all people with learning disabilities have dyslexia. A way to help dyslexic individuals read your online survey is to use the font called Read Regular. Read Regular is designed with an individual approach for each of the characters, creating difference in the actual characters and not mirroring letters. For example, the letter *b* is not mirrored to make the letter *d* in order to create a large character differentiation. The character shapes are simple and clear, creating consistency. The characters have been stripped down of all unnecessary details.

Ensuring That Participants Respond Only Once

Researchers need to be cautious of receiving completed questionnaires from the same respondent multiple times. The ethical norm of respondent anonymity and the practical goal of eliciting only one response per person are at odds with each other; however, there are some techniques for preventing or identifying duplicate responses. Assigning a unique identifier to each respondent is the most effective way to prevent people from entering multiple responses. Without using a unique identifier, there are no 100% effective techniques to prevent people from submitting more than one questionnaire. Other strategies include the following:

- Compare host names or Internet protocol (IP) addresses of submissions. Every computer on the Internet has a unique identifying number called the IP address. You must have some knowledge of how these addresses are assigned on each network to make effective use of this technique. Because network address translation (NAT) has grown in popularity, it is common for many computers to share a single IP address. NAT involves rewriting the source and/or destination addresses of IP packets as they pass through a router or firewall. Most systems using NAT do so in order to enable multiple hosts on a private network to access the Internet using a single public IP address. Setting up the survey to automatically reject multiple responses from the same IP address is possible but not recommended. Usually, automatic rejection will result in the rejection of valid responses and allow people to give multiple responses by moving to a different computer.

- Check for series of data that have identical answers to the question set. This should be used in combination with one of the other checks.
- Make a gateway survey to the actual survey that accepts a one-time-use password. These passwords will be logged separately from the data collected, so there will be no way to link this password with the responses.

Summary

Although some of the design principles applicable to paper questionnaires can be instructive for creating online questionnaires, Web-based surveys are unique and require careful consideration when it comes to layout, user friendliness, and technical requirements. A clear understanding of the demographic and Web usability profiles of the target audience will aid researchers in making appropriate choices about factors such as color, appearance, response options, and the amount and level of instructions necessary for particular surveys.

Online survey software and computer hardware are developing at breakneck pace, and the diffusion of computer technology in society is advancing equally rapidly. As more and more members of target populations become tech savvy and online surveys become the norm rather than a novelty, these guidelines for designing online questionnaires will require updating. It is incumbent on researchers using online data collection tools to keep track of the literature in the field and adjust their techniques for developing online survey instruments accordingly.

Note

1. If an organization or group is more commonly known by an acronym, such as the FBI, it is preferable to use the acronym on first reference. *Federal Bureau of Investigation* not only takes longer to read but may actually create more confusion than it clears up.

6

Conducting the Survey

Current research on Internet surveys has yet to provide a set of clear rules about effective fielding of electronic surveys; this is an area of social research methodology that is evolving and will continue to change as technology solves some problems and introduces new ones. Nevertheless, we provide some strategies for administering Internet surveys, including ways to maximize the response rate and safeguards to ensure that participants respond to each questionnaire only once.

Methods of Recruitment

There are several electronic methods that can be used to recruit participants. Each approach has advantages and disadvantages. These methods include

- an e-mail invitation,
- a link to the survey on a Web site, and
- an interstitial (pop-up) window.

An E-Mail Invitation

E-mail invitations require that you have the e-mail addresses of your target respondents. For example, if you want to survey attendees of a conference, members of an organization, or people who signed up to receive an online newsletter, there will be a list of the e-mail addresses of these individuals; your task will be to procure the list. If, however, your goal is to measure public opinion on a topic, this approach will not work; you should elect to post the survey on Web sites.

E-mail surveys can be distributed in one of three ways. One method is by sending the questionnaire as an attachment to an e-mail message. This method requires the recipient to open the attachment, save it, type in his or her answers, and then send the completed survey back to the sender. There is a chance that viruses can be spread using this method. This approach is not recommended because of the extra steps required of the potential participant and the risk of spreading viruses.

Second, the questionnaire can be embedded in the e-mail message itself. This method has the advantage of simplicity. The respondent can simply elect to "reply" to the message, type the answers into the e-mail, and hit the send button. The disadvantage is that the person cannot start the questionnaire and set it aside to finish later. Therefore, this approach should be used only for very short surveys. Other disadvantages are that the survey will have a very plain appearance and the use of images or tables will be limited. Additionally, the formatting of the survey can be disrupted when sent in this manner, and data entry is required; the data are not automatically added to a database. Anonymity is another concern as the respondent's e-mail addressed is associated with the completed survey. The lack of anonymity can cause the respondent to be less honest and can affect the validity and reliability of the responses.

The third, and preferred, approach is to include a link to the survey in the e-mail invitation. This makes the survey easily accessible, and all the "bells and whistles" of a Web-based survey can be utilized. It is also an interactive approach, is personal, and can provide the respondents with anonymity.

The advantages and disadvantages of e-mail surveys are given in Table 6.1.

Invitation Letters

Invitations, usually sent by e-mail, are the first point of contact with the potential respondent. This is an opportunity for the researcher to sell the survey. If the invitation is not enticing, then the reader is likely to delete the message, close the pop-up window, or discard the request. You need to persuade the recipient that the survey is a valuable way to spend his or her time.

The invitation should be intriguing, simple, and short. Elements such as tone, length, readability, respect for the respondent, and credibility of the researcher are important. The invitation needs to be friendly, respectful, motivating, and trustworthy; emphasize the importance and ease of responding;

and provide clear instructions as to how to proceed. The following are some suggestions:

- Keep it short and simple (a maximum of three paragraphs).
- Explain why the survey is important.
- Represent the survey accurately in terms of the purpose.
- The design and layout should be professional and visually appealing.
- Inform the reader of the approximate time needed to complete the survey.
- Make the language consistent with the survey and appropriate for the audience.
- Address the issues of confidentiality and anonymity.
- Include the company logo if you have one; it will build trust and credibility.
- Thank the reader in advance for giving his or her time for completing the survey.

Table 6.1   Advantages and Disadvantages of E-Mail Invitations

Advantages	Disadvantages
Fast response time	E-mail addresses of potential respondents are needed
Invitations are easy to distribute from one master e-mail list	Some participants may experience technological problems
Reminders are easy to send and can be sent multiple times	Data are representative of only those people whose e-mail address the researcher has; coverage bias exists
Can easily contact people with common interests or characteristics—for example, students enrolled at a college or members of a professional organization	May be viewed as spam mail and be deleted
Can contact the potential participant immediately after an interaction—for example, satisfaction questionnaires sent to customers right after the service date	Some potential respondents may not open the e-mail or the attachment due to concerns about the spread of viruses

Although invitations to participate in online surveys are usually sent by e-mail, they also can be delivered by postal mail. If you are posting your survey on a Web site, you can mail out the invitation letter and include the Web site address and password (if you are using one) in the body of the letter. Be sure that the Web address and password are easy to locate and stand out from the text of the letter; printing this information in bold text should be sufficient to accomplish this. The benefit of sending the invitation by mail is that you do not need the e-mail addresses of your potential participants. It also opens up the possibility of selecting a probability sample of respondents for the survey. The downside is that the recipient of the letter needs to take the time and go to the computer to complete the survey. The extra step can reduce your response rate. Sample invitation letters appear in Appendices D and E.

A Link on a Web Site

Banners and icons can be placed on Web sites asking people to complete the survey. The user clicks on the icon, and the invitation asks visitors to complete the survey. This method of recruiting respondents is for researchers who are seeking data from the general population or a specific target audience. Recall from our earlier discussion of sampling that to gather information from the general public, your survey can be advertised on a variety of popular Web sites. If you are targeting a more specific audience, then you will need to advertise your survey on related sites. For example, if you want to survey health care professionals, then you may choose to advertise your survey on several health-related sites. To use this method, you do not need the e-mail addresses of the potential respondents; however, it takes longer than e-mail surveys to get an adequate sample size. The advantages and disadvantages of this method are listed in Table 6.2.

Table 6.2   Advantages and Disadvantages of Invitations on Web Sites

Advantages	Disadvantages
E-mail addresses are not needed	Passive approach; visitors may not notice or be intrigued by the banner
The visitor may be more motivated to complete the survey as he or she has an interest in the topic, which is why the visitor is viewing the site—for example, a health-related Web site	Cooperation from other organizations is required if the researcher wants to post the survey on other Web sites
Can place the survey on other Web sites	Takes longer to obtain the desired sample size
Lets the respondent be proactive and is nonintrusive	Banners and icons need to attract the attention of the visitor and be visually appealing
Respondent may have trust in the organization, and the survey carries more credibility	May obtain a lower sample size
	Software may be installed on potential respondents' computers to block banners; if this type of software is installed, then the viewer may not see your request for participation

Regardless of your audience, you will want to entice respondents to complete your survey. The researcher can attract the reader by briefly describing the incentive (if there is one) in the banner. Bauman, Jobity, Airey, and Atak (2000) found that replacing a static image and adding a flashing bold red and blue text to the banner increased the response rate. After adding the flash to the icon, the hit rate on the icon increased by 32% and the completion rate nearly doubled.

Interstitial (Pop-Up) Window Invitations

An interstitial (something "in between") is a page that is inserted in the normal flow of editorial content structure on a Web site for the purpose of advertising or promotion. A separate window pops up while every visitor or every nth visitor is logged onto the Web page. It can be intrusive, and the reaction of viewers usually depends on how welcome or entertaining the message is. An interstitial is usually designed to move automatically to the page where the survey is located if the user clicks on the pop-up window. It is best to offer an incentive to motivate visitors to complete the survey. It is also a good idea to place the client's logo on the pop-up window so that it is not perceived as a pop-up from a third party and adds credibility. Bauman et al. (2000) tried the pop-up method, and the click rate was about 30% with a completion rate of 60%. The advantages and disadvantages of this method are outlined in Table 6.3.

There are presently hundreds of software programs on the market that are designed to block pop-ups, banner ads, spyware, and spam. Many of the programs will block basic pop-up and pop-under messages and play a sound, such as a beep (or whatever the user chooses), every time an ad is blocked. More sophisticated software allows users to block all forms of advertising, including Flash ads, messenger ads, and sponsored ads on Web sites like Google and Yahoo. Many programs also include automatic updates so that the product does not become outdated. Some ad blockers even include detailed statistics so that the user can view the number and types of ads blocked. This type of software is generally inexpensive or available for free downloading.

The proliferation of such programs is a clear indication that Web users are seeking ways to eliminate what they perceive to be annoying interruptions. As Web surfers increasingly adopt pop-up blocking software and switch to Web browsers and Internet service providers that claim to eliminate pop-up ads entirely, it will be incumbent on online survey researchers to supplement this method of recruiting respondents with additional techniques.

Table 6.3   Advantages and Disadvantages of Interstitial Windows

Advantages	Disadvantages
Gets the attention of the viewer	Viewer may not perceive the survey to be credible depending on what sites the pop-up windows appear on
E-mail addresses are not needed	Very intrusive; the viewer may be annoyed by the interruption
Forces a response from the visitor— they either have to complete the survey or close the window	Can irritate site visitors and cause them to leave the site
Can select a simple random or systematic (every *n*th) sample of visitors to a particular Web site	Software may be installed on the potential respondents' computer to block the pop-up window; if this type of software is installed, then the viewer may not see your request for participation
Draws the visitor's attention to the survey at the time of his or her viewing the site	
Can get a high response rate if the site is frequently visited	

Increasing the Response Rate

Obtaining high response rates can be challenging when conducting online survey research. Issues such as the construction of the survey invitation, follow-up contacts with nonrespondents, and incentives can have an impact and should be considered when conducting online surveys.

Follow-Up Invitations

Sending follow-up invitations can help increase the response rate and is encouraged. If you sent out the questionnaires via e-mail, then you most likely have created a distribution list containing the e-mail addresses of the sample respondents. You have two options for sending reminder e-mail invitations:

1. Sort the distribution list to remove addresses of participants who have already completed the questionnaire, and send the reminder to only those who have not yet responded.

2. Send reminders to everyone on the distribution list.

In the second case, it will be necessary to include a statement that reads, "If you have already completed and submitted your questionnaire, then please disregard this e-mail." Choosing this option presents the possibility that some respondents will complete the questionnaire a second time; they may forget that they have already participated or may believe that the second e-mail refers to a different survey. Because respondents are not anonymous in this situation, the problem can be overcome with vigilant checking of new e-mail addresses against those who have already responded.

If you are using a Web survey tool to administer your survey, the program will have features that allow you to easily import lists of e-mail addresses for the initial sending of e-mail invitations as well as for follow-up reminders. The Web survey hosts Zoomerang and SurveyMonkey allow developers to view the e-mail deployment history and send reminders to only those who have not responded. Sending reminders is usually a matter of hitting the "resend" button included with the "list management" features of the software. While the actual sending of the follow-up reminder invitations is a straightforward task, the timing of follow-ups should be carefully considered as it has been shown to make a difference in recipients' behavior.

Kittleson (1997) found that follow-up e-mails sent to potential participants of e-mail surveys increase the response rates. Kittleson sent an e-mail survey to 276 members selected from the International E-Mail Directory for Health Educators. The participants were divided into four groups. All groups received the survey on Day 1, and they were asked to complete the survey within 14 days. Group 1 did not receive a follow-up reminder. Group 2 was sent a follow-up reminder accompanied by the survey on Day 7. Group 3 was sent two follow-up reminders with the survey attached on Days 5 and 10. Group 4 was sent four follow-up reminders, each including the survey, on Days 3, 6, 9, and 12. Table 6.4 shows the results.

Based on these data, it appears that one follow-up message sent about 1 week after the initial e-mail invitation is optimal; the additional increase

Table 6.4   Response Rate of Four Groups Receiving an E-Mail Survey

	Group 1 (no follow-up)	Group 2 (one follow-up)	Group 3 (two follow-ups)	Group 4 (four follow-ups)
No. returned	19	36	39	37
Rate (%)	27.5	52.2	56.5	53.6

SOURCE: From Kittleson, M., Determining effective follow-up of e-mail surveys. In *American Journal of Health Behavior* 21(3), 193–196. Copyright © 1997, American Journal of Health Behavior www.ajhb.org. Used with permission of PNG Publications.

in response rate yielded by two or four follow-ups is negligible and fails to provide sufficient return for the researcher's investment in time.

The time of day that a reminder message is sent is also an important consideration. Granello and Wheaton (2004) conducted a Web-based survey research project to gather data on response patterns. Four hundred and nineteen responses were returned from the 1,136 people who received the survey announcement. Based on observations of the response patterns, the researchers found that sending reminders late in the day or early in the morning had the most effect in terms of increasing the response rate. The times of day when the highest number of responses was received were between 7:30 and 8:30 a.m. and between 3:30 and 4:30 p.m.

Using Behavioral Theory to Increase the Response Rates

A host of behavioral theories can be used to develop techniques for increasing response rates in online surveys. Theories of social exchange, cognitive dissonance, self-perception, and involvement provide useful insight into respondents' motivations and point to specific strategies for applied research (see Evangelista, Albaum, & Poon, 1999).

Social Exchange

Social exchange theory asserts that decisions to take action are evaluated in terms of costs and benefits—that is, people want to minimize costs and maximize benefits. When offered incentives, potential respondents will weigh the value of the incentive against their perceived cost in time and effort. Incentives come in two forms, material and nonmaterial.

Material Incentives. Material incentives for online surveys are not as easily distributed as those for mail survey incentives. It is not possible to mail a $5 bill over the Internet or to entice the potential respondent with a display of raffle items as when a survey is being conducted in a store, business, or shopping mall. This does not mean that incentives cannot be used. In fact, research shows that incentives are effective for increasing response rates for online surveys.

Incentives can be distributed in a number of ways. They can be mailed to the respondent, or the respondent may be able to print out a coupon or gift certificate after the completed survey is submitted. Another way is to give the respondent a code. The person can receive the discount or free gift when he or she logs onto a Web site and enters the code. If the survey is posted on a Web site, and you recruit participants by mailing out letters via the postal service, you can include the incentive with the letter. The incentives given for each respondent are usually of a lower monetary value than incentives for drawings, and incentives for shorter surveys usually have a lower monetary value than incentives for longer surveys.

There are many different types of incentives. Incentives, such as loyalty points or discount coupons, can be given to each respondent. Alternatively, respondents can be entered into a drawing for a highly desirable prize, such as a reserved parking space in a crowded parking lot. If given to each respondent, then whoever completes the survey will receive a gift. In the case of the drawing, only one respondent receives the prize, but the prize is of greater value than the individual gifts.

The choice of the incentive used needs to be considered carefully. There are a few special considerations when selecting your incentive for an online survey. Be sure that the incentive is truly one that will be relevant for all participants. For example, if your target audience is men, then offering an incentive for free nail polish may not be a good choice. If your target audience is students at a particular college or university, then a gift certificate for the bookstore is appropriate and valuable to the target audience. You also need to consider if your respondents will be international. Gift certificates for sites such as Amazon.com or an international bookstore are good choices if your target audience is dispersed geographically. You also could offer the respondent a choice from a specified list of incentives of equal value, but mailing packages all over the globe is not reasonable and can be costly.

You will need to think about the timeliness of your incentive. If you are going to raffle off school supplies but the drawing will be held in May, then you may want to reconsider your selection. If the survey is related to breast cancer, for example, then for each person who completes the survey, the company may donate a specified amount of money to a cancer nonprofit or research center. Using the same example, you may want to conduct the survey during the breast cancer awareness month.

A meta-analysis of incentive experiments conducted by Göritz (2005) revealed that incentives do motivate people to start a Web survey. Incentives increase the likelihood of a person responding to a survey by 19% relative to the odds without incentives. Incentives also increase the chance that the respondent will complete the survey rather than drop out by 27% relative to the odds without incentives. Göritz also found that promised nonmonetary incentives seem to be more effective in online than offline surveys. In a stand-alone study, Göritz (2004) found that the response rate when the incentive was loyalty points was slightly higher (82.4%) than if money (78%) or trinkets (78.6%) were raffled. If more loyalty points were offered, the drop-out rate was lower.

Nonmaterial Incentives. Offering nonmaterial incentives also can affect the response rates. Göritz (2005) conducted three online experiments and noted that when a summary of the survey results was offered the response rates were slightly higher than if the summary was not offered. Drop-out rates were also lower when a data summary was offered.

Convincing potential respondents that participation in the survey will be fun is another way to maximize their reward for taking part in the survey. Of course, it will then be incumbent on you to ensure that the survey really is fun.

Cognitive Dissonance

Cognitive dissonance can occur when our behaviors do not match our cognitions. It is an uncomfortable state, and individuals experiencing cognitive dissonance will take steps to reduce the dissonance. In the survey research setting, cognitive dissonance may arise if a respondent sees himself or herself as a "helpful" person but then refuses to participate in a survey. To reduce the dissonance (or inconsistency between self-perception and behavior), the potential respondent can take part in the survey. Survey invitations that mention that respondents will be "helping" the researcher or that "every response is essential to the accuracy of the data" can trigger cognitive dissonance in some individuals. Individuals who do not see themselves as helpful people will not be moved to participation by cognitive dissonance.

Self-Perception

The application of self-perception theory to online survey response relies on individuals' desire to view themselves as kind, helpful, and generous. By inviting people to participate in a survey, you are offering them an opportunity to manifest these qualities. Researchers can label the act of participation as "generous," thereby helping prospective respondents to classify themselves. The theory predicts that potential respondents who identify with the label will choose to participate.

Involvement

Involvement or commitment to a particular system, process, or organization can affect one's likelihood of participating in an online survey. The more involved one is, the more likely one is to participate. To take advantage of involvement as a motivator for participating in an online survey, researchers can point out the following, when appropriate, in the survey invitation:

- The respondent is being contacted because of his or her prior action (such as attending a conference, purchasing a product, or using a service).

- The respondent's participation has implications for the maintenance of or change in a system or process—for example, "Your responses will help the marketing team decide on the new logo."
- The respondent will benefit tangibly from participation—for example, "We will be purchasing new inventory control software for your division and need your feedback."

Thank-You Notes

Thank-you notes should always be sent. The respondent took the time to complete the survey; the researcher should show his or her appreciation by sending a thank-you note. Also, if the person completes a customer satisfaction survey, for example, it will reassure the respondent that his or her opinion will be taken seriously. If you are using a Web-based survey host, you can write a thank-you e-mail and have it sent automatically soon after the respondent completes the questionnaire. Another option is to wait until all the responses are returned and then send the thank-you message to the entire list at once.

Summary

Recruiting participants is essential for obtaining a good response rate. People have many demands on their time, so this is not an easy task. You will need to consider your target audience and resources and provide considerable thought into developing the tools used, such as the invitation letter, follow-up messages, incentives, and banners. Basically, you want to get the attention of potential respondents, show that your survey is valuable and a good investment of their time, demonstrate creditability, and make the survey simple for them to access and complete.

7

Processing and Analyzing the Survey Data

W hen planning a survey, it is necessary to consider the analyses that will be required of the report. Do you simply want to describe your group? Or is the goal to make inferences about a population? By considering data analysis as part of the survey-planning process, you will be more likely to collect data that will adequately address your objectives.

Most Web-based survey hosts permit users to conduct data analysis via their Web sites. Some hosts provide options for descriptive statistics only, others allow researchers to conduct more complex analyses, and almost all offer the ability to download data so that they may be imported and used in statistical software packages. In no situation will you have to compute statistics by hand. You will, however, need to decide which statistics to compute using software, and you will need to interpret the results of the analyses. This chapter outlines strategies for analysis planning and data management. We also cover some basic statistical concepts and commonly used statistical tests for the analysis of survey data. A more in-depth study of statistical techniques is beyond the scope of this book; however, we have included references to statistical texts in the resource guide in Appendix A.

Planning for Data Analysis

The plan for data analysis begins with survey objectives, continues with appropriate measurement (suitable questions on the survey), and ends with detailed specification of the statistical tests to be performed. Example 7.1 shows two objectives from the same survey project, the survey questions used for measurement, and the analysis plan for each.

Example 7.1

1. *Survey objective 1:* To determine whether guilt is induced in an individual when that individual perceives that he or she has acted incorrectly in an interpersonal situation

   Measurement (survey question): "You are taking care of your close friend Chris's dog. While Chris is on vacation, the dog runs away. How likely are you to feel guilty when Chris returns and asks what happened to the dog?" (Measured on a 0- to 10-point scale: 0 = not at all guilty, 10 = extremely guilty)

   Analysis plan: Combine the 14 questions that measure guilt into an index; present descriptive statistics of the index

2. *Survey objective 2:* To determine whether there is a gender difference in the level of guilt induced in males and females

   Measurement: Index of 14 guilt-inducing situations; gender variable (male/female)

   Analysis plan: A t test for differences in guilt index mean between males and females

---

By thinking ahead to your analysis plan, you can adjust your survey questions to ensure that the level of measurement is appropriate for the planned statistical tests. If, for example, you expect to conduct t tests (which require that data be measured at the interval level) and your questions are written to elicit nominal responses (yes/no), you will either have to rewrite the questions or rethink the analysis plan. It also may be useful to sketch the summary tables, charts, and graphs you expect to use in presenting your results. Previewing the form in which you would like to present your data allows you to choose the statistical technique most appropriate for providing results in the necessary format.

Most Web-based survey hosts will allow you to view descriptive summary statistics on their Web sites. If you will need more advanced statistical analysis, it is important to investigate the features available in the software or on the host Web site before signing up for a service. Complex software and high-end Web survey applications offer embedded statistical analyses packages, which permit users to conduct a wide variety of analyses. The more basic programs allow users to download data in an Excel spreadsheet, which can then be imported into a third-party statistical software package for analysis. This is not difficult (e.g., the SPSS wizard will take you step by step through importing data from Excel into SPSS) but does involve a few extra steps and introduces more opportunity for error in data handling. Some midrange online survey software programs allow users to download data directly in SPSS, SAS, or **Minitab** format; this is an attractive option for researchers desiring a higher level of analysis than can be accomplished with Excel alone as it eliminates the need to move data from one program to another.

Tracking the Surveys

It is necessary to keep track of the questionnaires as they are completed so that you can monitor response rate, send reminders to nonrespondents, and identify problematic data early in the process.

If you have chosen e-mail administration of your survey, you will need to track the surveys manually. As the questionnaires are returned, each one should be assigned a unique identification (ID) number. E-mail questionnaires require data entry and are therefore typically printed to facilitate the process. Identification numbers can be typed or written onto the printed questionnaires. Many researchers find it useful to create a return rate graph. The graph (see Figure 7.1) allows you to track the progress of the returns and decide when to send follow-up reminders. These graphs are most practical when the survey will be in the field for at least a week; overnight polls, however, hardly require the creation of a return rate graph.

Data collected by a Web-based survey host can be automatically tracked via the host's software. If you have used an e-mail distribution list for dissemination of the survey invitations, you will be able to view whether or not each individual recipient has responded. If you have posted your survey on a Web page or are using pop-up invitations, you will only be able to see how many respondents have completed the survey. Figure 7.2 shows an example of a survey recipient tracking screen. Of the 10 respondents to whom the survey was sent, 4 have completed the questionnaire, 4 have not, and 2 have declined to participate. Using this list, the researcher can select those individuals who have not responded and send them a second request.

Most survey hosts allow customers to view and download responses as frequently as they like. Some even offer "real-time" viewing of results—that is, every time another respondent has completed the questionnaire, you can update the results to view the changes. As with e-mail questionnaires, tracking the return rate of Web-based surveys allows you to see the speed with which responses are being returned and determine when to send follow-ups.

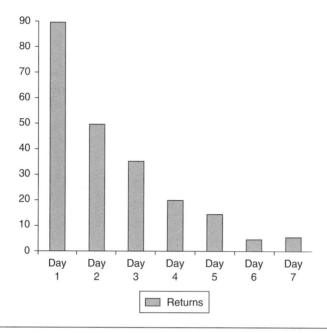

Figure 7.1   Return Rate Graph

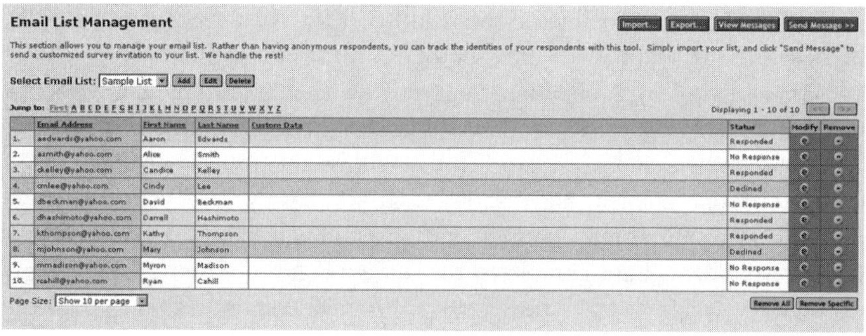

Figure 7.2   Tracking Report of E-mail Recipients

Creating a Codebook for E-Mail Surveys

Codebooks are guides to survey projects. They contain comprehensive documentation that enables other researchers who might subsequently want to analyze the data to do so without any additional information. A codebook provides information on the structure, contents, and layout of a data file.

Codebooks are essential for e-mail surveys as the questionnaire responses must be manually entered into a database. The idea is to translate all nonnumerical values on the questionnaire into numerical values (codes) that will be entered into the data file. For example, Question 1 on a survey asks, "Are you male or female?" You could assign to "male" the value of 1 and to "female" the value of 2. Note that these codes (1 and 2) are arbitrary; they could be anything that makes sense to the research team. The codebook is the document that lets everyone know that male = 1 and female = 2.

Some questions are precoded. For example, if you ask respondents how many times in the past week they ate at fast-food restaurants, the number they give you does not need to be translated further; you would enter whatever the respondents reported on the questionnaire. Similarly, if you asked about respondents' age in an open-ended question, you would enter whatever the respondents recorded. Figure 7.3 is an e-mail questionnaire, and Figure 7.4 is its codebook.

Although codebooks are not necessary for data entry purposes in Web-based surveys (because the data file is created automatically when respondents type in their answers), many Web survey programs have the option of creating codebooks that can be printed. These codebooks serve as a useful reference as you analyze the data and prepare the survey report.

Codebook Contents

While codebooks vary widely in quality and the amount of information given, a typical codebook includes

- ID numbers;
- variable name;
- variable description;
- variable format (i.e., number, text, date);
- codes used to indicate nonresponse and missing data;
- the exact questions and skip patterns used in a survey; and
- other indications of the content and characteristics of each variable.

Codebooks also may contain

- frequencies of response;
- survey objectives;
- concept definitions;
- a description of the survey design and methodology;
- a copy of the survey questionnaire (if applicable);
- information on data collection, data processing, and data quality; and
- information on how to handle illogical responses.

Student Learning Questionnaire

Thank you for taking the time to answer our survey. Your responses are important to us. Please complete this survey by clicking the **reply** button of your email program and filling in the answers to the questions. For multiple choice questions, just type an X in the brackets next to your answer; for other types of questions fill in your response in the brackets next to the question.

Thank you.

___

1. **How many times this year have you been involved in a group learning experience?**

   [ ] never   [ ] once   [ ] 2-3 times   [ ] 4-5 times   [ ] more than 5 times

2. **Overall, how would you rate your group learning experiences?**

   [ ] very positive   [ ] positive   [ ] undecided   [ ] negative   [ ] very negative

3. **When working in groups do you usually find yourself in a leadership position?**

   [ ] yes   [ ] no

4. **How easy or difficult is it for you to communicate your thoughts to the group?**

   [ ] very easy   [ ] easy   [ ] unsure   [ ] difficult   [ ] very difficult

5. **What size team do you prefer to work in?**

   [ ] 2 person   [ ] 3 person   [ ] 4 person   [ ] 5 person   [ ] 6 or more person

6. **What do you like most about working in groups? [   ]**

7. **What do you like least about working in groups? [   ]**

8. **What is your gender?**

   [ ] Male   [ ] Female

9. **What is your age? [   ]**

___

Figure 7.3   Example of an E-Mail Questionnaire

Student Learning Questionnaire–Codebook

Thank you for taking the time to answer our survey. Your responses are important to us. Please complete this survey by clicking the **reply** button of your email program and filling in the answers to the questions. For multiple choice questions, just type an X in the brackets next to your answer; for other types of questions fill in your response in the brackets next to the question.

Thank you.

---

1. **How many times this year have you been involved in a group learning experience?**

    1 never   **2** once   **3 2-3** times   **4 4-5** times   **5** more than **5** times

2. **Overall, how would you rate your group learning experiences?**

    1 very positive   **2** positive   **3** undecided   **4** negative   **5** very negative

3. **When working in groups do you usually find yourself in a leadership position?**

    1 yes   **2** no

4. **How easy or difficult is it for you to communicate your thoughts to the group?**

    1 very easy   **2** easy   **3** unsure   **4** difficult   **5** very difficult

5. **What size team do you prefer to work in?**

    1 2 person   **2 3** person   **3 4** person   **4 5** person   **5 6** or more person

6. **What do you like most about working in groups? [enter response]**

7. **What do you like least about working in groups? [enter response]**

8. **What is your gender?**

    1 Male   **2** Female

9. **What is your age? [enter response]**

Figure 7.4   Example of an E-Mail Questionnaire Codebook

Data Cleaning

Before data analysis can proceed, the survey data should be cleaned. Sources of "dirty" data include data entry errors (from e-mail surveys), incomplete answers, illogical answers, answers out of the possible range, and respondents selecting more answers than are allowable. Data cleaning is the process of identifying and correcting these errors. *Warning:* Data cleaning does *not* mean throwing out answers that don't support your research objectives. It is important not to let your goals get in the way of what the data actually say.

Data cleaning is needed regardless of what type of online survey methodology you use; e-mail surveys require the most and Web-based surveys require the least amount of data cleaning. E-mail questionnaires must be hand entered into a database (such as an Excel spreadsheet or directly into an analysis program such as SPSS) and are therefore prone to typos. When using Web-based surveys, you will need to screen the data file for impossible answers such as those that are out of the possible range—for example, someone reporting that he or she is 156 years old. If the Web survey host you are using has a "skip logic" feature (almost all do), the issue of illogical answers—for example, male respondents reporting that they have been pregnant—will not be a problem.

Data Cleaning as a Process

Data cleaning deals with data problems once they have occurred. Error prevention strategies, such as writing clear questions, providing instructions for answering, and programming questionnaires to automatically skip irrelevant questions, can reduce many problems but cannot eliminate them. Although you may encounter data errors incidentally throughout the analysis process, it is advisable to perform systematic data cleaning before commencing with analysis. Van den Broeck, Argeseanu Cunningham, Eeckels, and Herbst (2005) presented data cleaning as a three-stage process, involving screening, diagnosing, and editing of suspected data abnormalities.

Step 1: Screening Phase

Data screening formally begins when most of the data have been entered (or downloaded from a Web survey host) and analysts can start to scan spreadsheets and summary tables. The screening can begin earlier, however, as soon as the first questionnaires are returned. Checking the questionnaires early sometimes allows researchers to catch problems and rectify them before the research is too far under way. For example, suppose you begin to screen returned questionnaires as soon as they are completed and you see the same block of missing answers on all of them. You investigate and discover that a skip pattern was incorrectly programmed. You would have time to fix the error and continue with the fielding of the survey.

At the screening level, look for patterns of missing data, inconsistencies in the data, strange patterns in the distributions, and extreme values (**outliers**). In addition to scanning the data file, researchers also can create frequency distribution tables and graphs to look for odd data points.

Step 2: Diagnostic Phase

The purpose of the diagnostic phase is to identify the cause of the strange data points. Some values may be clearly impossible—for example, a respondent reporting that she watched 25 hours of television yesterday. Others will be unlikely—such as a college student reporting that he is 12 years old. Possible causes of these odd data points include the following: incorrect data entry by data entry personnel in the case of e-mail surveys or respondent error in the case of Web-based surveys (perhaps the college student respondent meant to type in *21* instead of *12* and transposed the numbers); the question may have been misunderstood; or the data may be real (the unlikely, not the impossible data).

Step 3: Treatment Phase

After you identify errors, missing and strange values, and true but extreme data, you will need to decide what to do about the problematic observations. Impossible values are the easiest to tackle. If you can find the correct value by returning to the original e-mail questionnaire or by following up with respondents if the survey was not anonymous, then you should be able to fix the data. If it is not possible to ascertain the real value because you have conducted an anonymous Web-based survey, then you should delete the value.

When it comes to possible but unlikely values, the options are less clear. Some statisticians recommend that extreme values should always remain in the data file unchanged. Others suggest statistical treatments such as imputation (e.g., replacing the value with the group mean for that variable). A third school of thought permits the deletion of extreme values so long as it is noted in the final report that some values were "excluded from the analysis." The overriding concern here is with accurate and ethical data analysis and reporting. When a researcher begins to toss out data, there is danger that the integrity of the data set will be compromised. It is best to evaluate extreme data points on a case-by-case basis and reserve the option of deleting unlikely cases as a last resort.

Data Transformation

Once the data have been entered and cleaned, it is almost always necessary to transform some of the raw data into variables that are usable in the analyses. For example, if you collected information about respondents' age by asking for the date of birth, you will have to do some arithmetic to transform the data into age in years. Other issues such as missing values on some questions and the need to recode some scales must be addressed before data analysis can begin.

Missing Values

Many analysis programs automatically treat questions without a response in the data file as missing values. In others, you need to define specific codes to represent missing values. For instance, you might use a value of 99 to indicate that the respondent did not enter an answer for that question. It is important to check the specifications of the analysis program you are using to determine how missing values are handled.

Recording Data

Before analyzing the data, you may need to recode some scale items so that all the response options are consistent. For instance, let's say you had a 5-point response scale for a self-esteem measure where 1 meant strongly disagree and 5 meant strongly agree. One item is "I generally feel good about myself." If the respondent strongly agrees with this item, he or she will enter a 5, and this value would be indicative of higher self-esteem. Alternatively, consider an item such as "Sometimes I feel like I'm not worth much as a person." Here, if a respondent strongly agrees by rating this 5, it would indicate low self-esteem. To compare these two items, we would reverse the scores of one of them (we'd probably reverse the latter item so that high values will always indicate higher self-esteem). If the original value was 1, change it to 5, 2 is changed to 4, 3 remains the same, 4 is changed to 2, and 5 is changed to 1. While you could program these changes as separate statements in most programs, it's easier to do this with a simple formula, for example,

New Value = (High Value + 1) − Original Value

In our example, the High Value for the scale is 5, so to get the new (transformed) scale value, we simply subtract each Original Value from 6 (i.e., 5 + 1). Many statistical programs have the capability to transform data from several questions for all the surveys with a few easy key strokes.

Descriptive Statistics

Descriptive statistics are used to describe the basic features of the data in a study. They provide summaries about the sample characteristics and responses to individual survey questions. Together with simple tables and charts, descriptive statistics form the basis for quantitative data analysis.

Descriptive statistics are typically distinguished from inferential statistics. Whereas descriptive statistics are used to describe what's going on in a data set, inferential statistics are used to make statements beyond the sample data. For example, we might use inferential statistics to try to make inferences about public opinion in a large population of voters based on data from a random sample.

The first step in any data analysis strategy is usually to look at each questionnaire item individually. There are two convenient ways to do this: (a) run frequency distributions for each question and (b) compute summary statistics for each question.

Frequency Distributions

The frequency distribution of a particular questionnaire item shows the numbers (and/or percentages) of respondents who selected each response option. The distribution of values can be presented in tables or graphs. Almost all Web-based survey hosts include the option of creating frequency distributions and presenting them as either tables or bar charts. These basic frequency distributions are usually the default mode in which online survey software hosts present results. The function can be found in the host's "analysis" or "analyze" menu. Table 7.1 shows a frequency distribution presented as a table. It reveals that the majority of this sample were junior and senior students; there were a few sophomores (six) and graduate students (five) and only two freshmen. Figure 7.5 is a horizontal bar graph displaying answers to an employee job satisfaction question. Viewed this way, readers can see at a glance that the majority of the sample reported being "satisfied" with their jobs.

Another useful way to quickly view the results of a particular question is to construct a chart, such as the one in Figure 7.6. This pie chart reports the percentages rather than the number of students answering in each category. It is easy to see that the majority of students reported fulfilling "transfer requirements" as the reason they chose to take an online course.

Summary Statistics

Summary statistics are designed to provide concise descriptions of the distributions of answers to survey questions. Distributions are often described

Table 7.1   Frequency Distribution Table

Class Level	Frequency	Percentage	Cumulative Percentage
Freshman	2	3.7	3.7
Sophomore	6	11.1	14.8
Junior	23	42.6	57.4
Senior	18	33.3	90.7
Graduate student	5	9.3	100.0
Total	54	100.0	

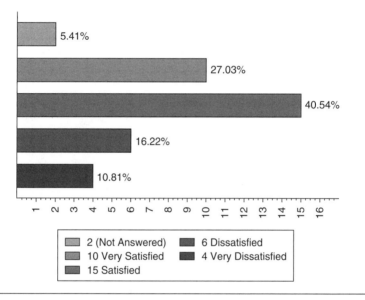

Figure 7.5   Bar Graph

using two summary statistics: mean and **standard deviation**. The mean is the average, a measure of central tendency. The standard deviation of a distribution tells us about variability, roughly how much, on average, the values differ from the mean. Other useful summary statistics are the **median**—the midpoint of a distribution, the **mode**—the most frequently occurring value, and the range—the distance between the smallest and the largest value in the distribution. (See Appendix F for a review of the computation of these summary statistics.) The basic-level Web survey hosts do not routinely provide

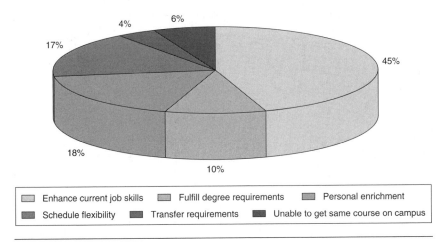

Figure 7.6   Pie Chart

summary statistics but sometimes offer users the ability to upgrade their service (for an additional charge) so that they can compute these statistics. An alternative is to export the raw data as an Excel spreadsheet and compute summary statistics in Excel.

Cross-Tabulation

After looking at the frequency distributions and summary statistics of individual questions, you may next want to examine two variables at a time. Many of the survey software and Web-based programs allow researchers to create cross-tabulation tables. The cross-tabulation is a table wherein the responses to one question are displayed in the rows and the responses to another question are displayed in the columns. For example, let's say you asked the following two questions in an online survey:

1. "If you are a health care provider, what is your specialty?"
2. "Do you intend to offer continuing education courses?"

You may want to know how which types of health care providers intend to offer continuing education courses. A cross-tabulation would provide this information in a table, and it is easily accessible in most programs by using a few key strokes. Figure 7.7 shows the results of this cross-tabulation.

If you are a health care provider, what is your specialty?				
		Do you intend to offer continuing education courses?		
	Total	Yes	No	Not Sure
Total	8	1	4	3
Cardiology	0	0	0	0
Dentistry	0	0	0	0
Dermatology	0	0	0	0
Endocrinology	0	0	0	0
Internal Med.	1	1	0	0
Mental Health	4	0	3	1
Nephrology	0	0	0	0
Ophthalmology	0	0	0	0
Otolaryngology	0	0	0	0
Optometry	0	0	0	0
Pediatrics	0	0	0	0
Psychiatrist	0	0	0	0
Urology	0	0	0	0
Other	3	0	1	2

Figure 7.7   Cross-Tabulation Results

Filters

Another way to examine survey responses in order to detect patterns in results is to apply filters to questions. For example, you may want to look at only the answers from female respondents for a certain question; in this case, you would filter out the data provided by male respondents. Figure 7.8 is an example of a filter definition frame. Demographic and categorical variables such as job title, political party affiliation, or product preference are commonly used to filter responses. Although the cross-tabulation procedure described above also allows users to look at responses based on category membership, applying filters isolates the category of interest, allowing for more specific investigation into a subset of the responses.

Inferential Statistics

After you have described your data using frequency distributions, summary statistics, and cross-tabulations, you may wish to determine whether differences exist between two or more groups of respondents. For example, you may want to know whether males and females differ on an opinion question.

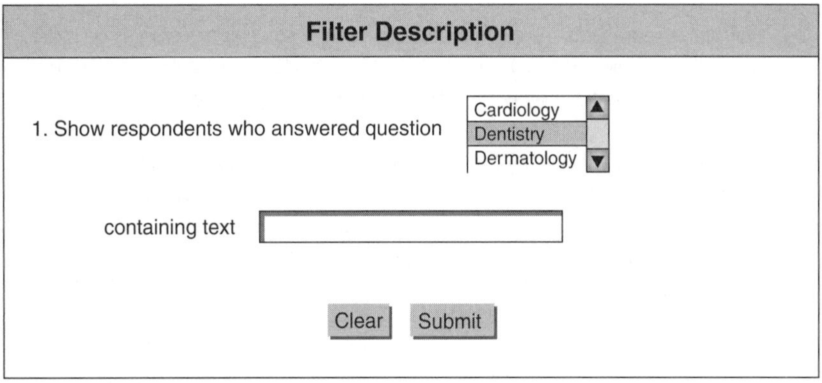

Filter Description

1. Show respondents who answered question

Cardiology
Dentistry
Dermatology

containing text

Clear   Submit

Figure 7.8   Applying a Filter

Or, perhaps, you may want to make a statement about the population from which the sample was drawn. The statistical method you choose to compare respondents is determined by the number and type of variables you are comparing. When comparing two nominal (categorical) variables, use the chi-square test. When comparing the means of two random samples, a *t* test is appropriate. And when evaluating the relationship between two interval variables, you could conduct a **correlation** analysis. You will be able to conduct these analyses only by exporting your raw data into a statistical analysis software package such as SPSS, SAS, or Minitab. Off-the-shelf Web survey software solutions usually do not have the capability to perform these tests. If you determine that you will need to conduct *t* tests, correlation analysis, or something more advanced such as analysis of variance or multiple regression, it may be worthwhile to invest in software that allows direct export of raw data into the statistical analysis package of your choice or consider an inclusive package that provides a Web survey development application and advanced data analysis software.

A Note About Alpha and *p* Values

When researchers write "the results of the test were statistically significant at a significance level of .05 (*p* < .05)," they are saying that the relationship described by the observed test statistic is not likely due to chance. More specifically, the likelihood that the relationship is due to chance is less than 5%. The .05 is referred to as alpha. There is nothing sacred about the .05; it is one frequently used alpha level; .01 is another commonly used alpha level.

A *p* **value** represents the probability of seeing results as extreme as or more extreme than those actually observed if in fact there was no relationship between the variables you're testing. Statistical software routinely provides *p* values associated with statistical tests—for example, *p* = .027. Traditionally, the *p* values of a test have been compared with a predetermined alpha level. If the *p* value was greater than alpha, then it would be concluded that the results of the test were "not significant"; if the *p* value was less than or equal to the predetermined alpha level, then one could conclude that there was a "statistically significant" relationship between the variables. (See Example 7.2.)

Example 7.2

p = .003, <.05: The *p* value is less than alpha; there is a statistically significant relationship between the variables.

p = .214, alpha < .05: The *p* value is greater than alpha; there is no statistically significant relationship between the variables.

This type of analysis is called fixed-level testing, because the researcher determines the acceptable level of alpha before analysis begins. Many contemporary statisticians have moved away from fixed-level testing and the language of "statistical significance." One reason is that reporting the significance of a test using a predetermined alpha without citing the *p* value limits the reader's ability to fully interpret the results. For example, if a report claims that the results of a test show a statistically significant relationship using alpha .05, the *p* value could have been .049 or .001 (or anything in between). In the first case, the results are just barely significant; in the second, they are wildly so.

A second concern about fixed-level testing is about the use of the term *significant*. Some researchers worry that readers will confuse the concepts of statistical significance and practical significance. As we have seen, statistical significance means that we are certain (to a specified degree) that our results are not due to chance. Practical significance, on the other hand, is a subjective judgment about the importance or usefulness of a finding.

Although there are good reasons to simply report *p* values associated with statistical tests, it is still common practice in many social scientific disciplines and applied research settings to predetermine alpha levels and state conclusions about statistical significance.

Chi Square

Nominal data were described earlier in this text as data that fall into unordered categories, such as the response options for gender, occupation, or city. To compare two questions each measured with nominal response options, you can create a contingency table that shows the categories to which each respondent belongs and conduct a chi-square test to determine whether a relationship between variables exists. Specifically, a chi-square test will examine the observed frequencies in a category and compare them with the expected frequencies in the same categories. The observed frequencies are the data collected by the survey. The expected frequencies are the values that would occur if chance alone were operating or if there was no relationship between the variables. If the questions are independent of each other, then the results of the chi-square test will be "nonsignificant," meaning that we believe that there is no relationship between the questions. If the questions are found to be related, then the results of the test will be "significant," suggesting that there is some relationship between the variables.

It is important to note that the results of a chi-square test tell us only if a relationship exists between two nominal variables; they do not inform us about the nature of the relationship. That is, we cannot make statements about causation (i.e., one variable is the cause of another). An example of a chi-square table is presented in Example 7.3.

Example 7.3

A researcher is interested in examining if there is a relationship between the gender of respondents and whether they favor or oppose a ballot proposition. The following contingency table was created based on the survey data. Cell contents are frequencies of responses in each category.

	Favor	Oppose	No Opinion
Male	10	17	26
Female	13	9	5

NOTE: Chi square = 11.0488, $p < .005$.

Looking at the table in Example 7.3, we can see that a relationship seems to exist, more women than men favor the position, and more men than women said they had "no opinion." The chi-square statistic noted below the table and its associated significance level (noted by $p < .005$) confirms that a relationship between gender and one's opinion on this proposition does exist. Put another way, there is a very small chance that these two variables are independent.

t Test

The *t* test compares the means of two groups and determines whether those two means are different enough to be statistically significant. It is an appropriate statistical test if you are examining the means of independent samples taken from two populations and if either the sample sizes are relatively large ($N > 30$) or you can assume that the data have roughly a bell-shaped or "normal" distribution. For example, say you wanted to determine if Republicans differed from Democrats on an authoritarian personality inventory. Party identification (Republican/Democrat) would be the grouping variable and score on the authoritarian personality inventory (from 0 to 100: 100 indicates a highly authoritarian personality) would be the test variable. The means on the personality inventory would be computed for each group and compared. If the means turned out to be significantly different (determined by the value of the test statistic), then we would say that the authoritarian personality scores of the Democrats and Republicans are statistically significantly different. The direction of the difference (which group was more authoritarian on average) is determined by looking at the means of the two groups.

Example 7.4 displays a portion of the computer output showing the results of a *t* test comparing the amount of guilt men and women said they would feel in a variety of interpersonal situations.

Example 7.4

Group Statistics

	Gender	N	Mean	Standard Deviation
Guilt	Male	21	96.0476	29.26854
	Female	45	112.0000	17.07337

The first step is to examine the descriptive statistics for the two groups. We see that the mean for females is higher (112.0000) than the mean for males (96.05476). On average, women in this sample reported that they felt more guilt than did the men. (The column labeled "*N*" in the table indicates the number of respondents in each category, and the last column contains the standard deviations for each group.)

Example 7.4 Continued

t Test for Equality of Means

t	*df*	*Significance (two tailed)*	*Mean Difference*	*Standard Error Difference*	*95% Confidence Interval of the Difference*	
					Lower	*Upper*
−2.320	26.552	.028	−15.952	6.875	−30.070	−1.834

We know based on the previous table that there is a difference in the sample means for men and women, but we don't know if that difference is significant. The second table in Example 7.4 shows a *t* statistic of −2.320 (see the first column of the table) and a significance level (*p* value) of .028 (third column of the table). From this, we could conclude that the mean amount of guilt reported by females in the sample was significantly higher than the mean amount of guilt reported by the male respondents. Using the fixed-level testing approach with alpha set at .05, you could report the results as follows: "Female respondents had higher guilt scores (*M* = 112.00, *SD* = 17.07) than male respondents (*M* = 96.05, *SD* = 29.7), *t* (27) = −2.320, *p* < .05." Using the *p*-value approach, most of the sentence would remain the same, but the last element would read, "*p* = .028."

Pearson Correlation

The Pearson product-moment correlation coefficient (Pearson correlation or just correlation) is used to determine the degree of the linear relationship between two interval variables. If there is a high degree of linear relationship, either positively or negatively, then a "linear" equation (straight line) based on one variable can be used to accurately predict the other. When discussing sample data, the Pearson correlation coefficient is denoted with the lowercase letter *r*. The value of *r* ranges from −1 to 1. An *r* of −1 indicates a perfect negative relationship, 0 means that no relationship exists between the variables, and 1 indicates a perfect positive relationship. These relationships are depicted in Figures 7.9, 7.10, and 7.11.

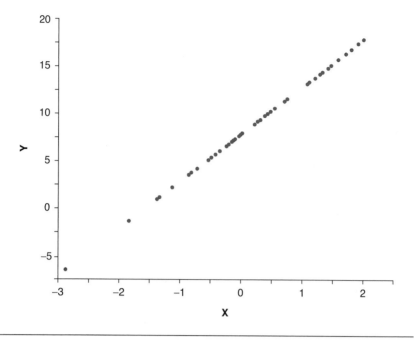

Figure 7.9   Perfect Positive Relationship Between *x* and *y*

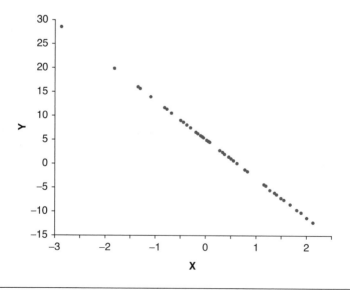

Figure 7.10   Perfect Negative Relationship Between *x* and *y*

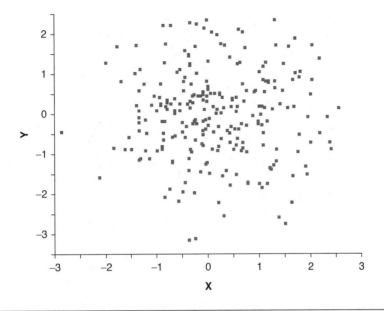

Figure 7.11   No Relationship Between *x* and *y*

Example 7.5

Suppose you are interested in the relationship between age (measured in years by an open-ended question) and attitude toward technology (measured with a 20-item scale: 0 = negative attitude toward technology, 20 = positive attitude toward technology). Because these are two interval variables, we can compute a correlation coefficient. The computer output looks like this:

	Age	*TECHATT*[a]
Age	1	−.331**
Significance (two tailed)		.007
N		68
TECHATT	−.331**	1
Significance (two tailed)	.007	
N	68	

NOTE: a. TECHATT = attitude toward technology.

**Correlation is significant at the .01 level (two tailed).

The correlation coefficient, *r*, in Example 7.5 is −.331, and the *p* value is .007. From this, we can conclude that there is a significant negative relationship between age and attitude toward technology: As age increases, attitude toward technology decreases, on average.

Earlier, we noted that responses to opinion scale items (e.g., strongly disagree to strongly agree) are commonly treated in analysis as interval data; therefore, we can compute correlation coefficients when examining opinion questions. Consider political ideology (measured on a liberal to conservative scale) and opinion on the death penalty. Example 7.6 shows the correlation matrix for these two questions. (Prior to this analysis, the scales were recoded so that higher numbers on the ideology variable indicates more liberal and higher numbers on the death penalty question indicates more strongly opposed to the death penalty.)

Example 7.6

	Ideology	*Death Penalty*
Ideology	1	.494**
Significance (two tailed)		.000
N		195
Death penalty	.494**	1
Significance (two tailed)	.000	
N	195	

NOTE: **Correlation is significant at the .01 level (two tailed).

Reading the results from the table in Example 7.6, we can see that there is a positive and statistically significant relationship (r = .494, p < .01) between being liberal and opposing the death penalty: As liberalness increases, so does opposition to the death penalty, on average. In this example and in Example 7.5, both correlation coefficients were significant (at the .01 level) but also relatively small (not very close to –1 or 1). This may leave you wondering about the proper way to interpret the size of correlation coefficients. In fact, the value of the correlation coefficient necessary for significance depends on the sample size (the larger the sample size, the less extreme the correlation coefficient needs to be to infer a significant correlation). Some authors (Babbie, 2004; Fink, 2003) provide the following general guidelines:

r = 0 to .25 (or –.25), which means little or no relationship.

r = .26 to .50 (or –.26 to –.50), which means a fair degree of relationship.

r = .51 to .75 (or −.51 to −.75), which means a moderate to good relationship.

r = more than .75 (or −.75), which means a very good to excellent relationship.

This is a handy rule of thumb but sometimes not so useful in practical applications. As we saw in the previous two examples, both coefficients were in the "fair-degree-of-relationship" range, not very impressive by some standards. If, however, we take note of the p value associated with each correlation coefficient (.007 in Example 7.5 and .000 in Example 7.6), the picture is different; both correlations are significant, most likely because they are both based on large ($N > 30$) samples. Interpreting correlation coefficients is largely situational; the reader must consider the value of r and the size of the sample from which r was computed.

Summary

We have covered much ground in this chapter, including the importance of thinking ahead to data analysis as you are planning your survey objectives, tracking respondents, coding and cleaning data, and preparing data for analysis, and finally, we have touched on some basic descriptive and inferential statistics that may be useful in preparing your survey report.

If you are familiar with basic statistics, much of what we have covered in the later part of this chapter would have been a review for you; if you are new to data analysis, this material may have been less accessible. It is important to underscore the point that this chapter does not provide enough detail for the survey researcher who wishes to conduct complex analysis of survey data. For that we recommend that you take a statistics course or consult with a survey statistician before beginning your project.

Our aim in this chapter has been to arm you with enough information so that you will be able to communicate your needs clearly should you choose to consult with a data analyst and so that you may effectively interpret data output if it is provided by your Web survey host.

8

Reporting the Survey Results

S urvey results can be presented in writing, orally, or both and often incorporate pictures, graphs, tables, and diagrams to visually present the findings. Although venues for research presentation in the academic and commercial worlds are greatly varied, there are some basic principles that will help researchers present the results of their online survey clearly and accurately. In this chapter, we discuss the essential components of written reports, oral presentations, and poster presentations and how to effectively communicate using visual aids.

Preliminary Considerations

Before beginning to write, it is important to consider your audience—that is, who will read your report? If the survey report is to be prepared for an academic audience, such as conference participants or journal editors, there will be strict guidelines with respect to length, citation style, and data presentation. Be certain to have these guidelines handy as you prepare your report. Additionally, you will want to use language appropriate for the intended audience. For example, discipline-specific jargon, which might be inappropriate for a lay audience, may very well be expected in an academic or technical venue.

On the other hand, if your readers will not have the requisite background to comprehend jargon, you should avoid the use of technical terms. Similarly, complex graphic illustrations of data and/or research methods should be avoided if the audience is not expert in your field or in survey research methods.

Format of a Survey Report

A written report is often disseminated at the end of a survey research project. The report should be comprehensive, well organized, and clearly written. Careful organization of a research paper will allow people to read your work selectively. When people read a survey report, they may have different interests—that is, one person may be interested in just the methods, whereas another reader may want to see a summary of the paper to determine if it is relevant to his or her study. The following is a list of the typical components of survey reports:

- Title page
- Acknowledgments
- Abstract or executive summary
- Table of contents
- List of tables
- List of figures
- Glossary or list of operational definitions
- Introduction
- Methods
- Results
- Discussion and recommendations
- References
- Appendix

The same format is generally used for journal articles, with the exception of tables of contents and lists of tables and figures. Executive summaries are usually included in technical/commercial reports; abstracts are the norm for academic papers. Usually, either an abstract or an executive summary is included, not both.

Many publishers have a specific format in which they want the work to be submitted, such as in the American Psychological Association (APA) or the Modern Language Association (MLA) style. APA style is used in many social science and related fields, such as anthropology, communication, education, linguistics, political science, psychology, and sociology. MLA publication guidelines are used in the humanities: philosophy, history, literature, and rhetoric. Determining the publisher's preferred style is usually simply a matter of consulting the publisher's Web site.

Title Page

Include the title of your study, your name, the organization that you are affiliated with or that sponsored the study, and the date of the report.

Acknowledgments

This is your opportunity to acknowledge the people who have contributed to the study and who have supported you in both professional and personal aspects of your life. If the research was funded, the sponsoring agency should be mentioned here.

Abstract

An abstract is a concise one- or two-paragraph summary of the completed work. Word limits for abstracts are usually between 100 and 200 words. In a minute or less, a reader can learn about the sample who participated in the study, the rationale behind the study, the general approach to the problem, pertinent results, and important conclusions or new questions. Write your abstract after the rest of the paper has been written. After all, how can you summarize something that is not yet written? Being clear and concise is important throughout any paper but especially in an abstract. Include the following elements in the abstract:

- The purpose of the study—hypothesis, overall research question, or objective(s)
- A brief description of the characteristics of the sample
- A brief description of the survey research
- Results, including limited but specific data
- Important conclusions or questions that follow from the study

The abstract should be written in the past tense. The focus should be on summarizing the results, and background information should be limited. The information in the abstract must be consistent with what is contained in the paper.

Executive Summary

The executive summary highlights the key points of the purpose and rationale of the study, the methodology, and key findings. There is more detailed information in the summary than in the abstract, and it is longer than the abstract, usually about one page in length. It is usually not necessary to include both an abstract and an executive summary. Academic reports typically require abstracts, while executive summaries are more appropriate for commissioned survey projects.

Table of Contents

This is a list of all major sections in the report and their associated page numbers.

List of Tables and List of Figures

This is a list of all the tables and figures in the report and their associated page numbers.

Introduction

The introduction is the beginning of the paper, and it should entice your audience to continue to read the paper. The purpose of an introduction is to acquaint the reader with the rationale behind the study and why your study is important. Try to keep your introduction brief. Your readers will want to quickly get to the body of the paper. The introduction places your work in a theoretical context and enables the reader to understand and appreciate your objectives. The introduction should

- describe the purpose of your study,
- describe the importance (significance) of the study—why it was worth doing in the first place (provide a broad context),
- explain why you used this particular theory or model and what are its advantages (you might comment on its suitability from a theoretical point of view as well as indicate the practical reasons for using it),
- provide a rationale (state your specific hypothesis(es) or objective(s) and describe the reasoning that led you to select them),
- very briefly describe the research design and how it accomplished the stated objectives, and
- provide a brief overview of the literature specifically related to your survey research project.

Glossary or Operational Definitions

This is where you define all technical terms or terms open to misinterpretation—for example, e-health, job aid, networks. You also should indicate what the abbreviations used in the paper stand for and explain their meanings. This information is usually included in the paper with the introduction.

Methods

The methods section describes what was done, who was involved, and how it was done. The procedure by which you conducted the study should be explained so that another individual could reproduce the study or judge the scientific merit of your work. It should not be a step-by-step description of everything you did or a set of instructions. In this section, you should describe

- the type of survey used;
- the limitations of the online survey methodology;
- the survey questions (give examples and include a copy in the appendix if you cannot include all the questions in the paper);
- the types of response categories—that is, drop-down menus, checklists, open ended;
- the distribution methods: how the survey was distributed, how the participants were recruited, how the nonrespondents were handled (that is, were follow-up e-mails sent and, if so, how many and when, how long was the online survey posted?);
- information about incentives if any were offered;
- how the survey was pilot tested;
- how reliability and validity were addressed;
- how the survey was constructed (that is, what languages was it available in, what software program was used, what was the reading level, were graphs incorporated?);
- how many people were e-mailed the survey, where you obtained their e-mail addresses from, what were the eligibility criteria;
- if the survey was anonymous;
- how you handled incomplete surveys; and
- how informed consent was handled.

Results

The purpose of a results section is to present and illustrate your findings. Make this section a straightforward report of the results, and save all interpretation for the discussion section of the report. Most survey results can effectively be presented using figures and tables. The content of this section should include

- a summary of your findings, illustrated, if appropriate, with figures and tables;
- a description of each of your results, noting the observations that are most relevant;
- a context, such as describing the research hypothesis that was addressed by a particular analysis; and
- an analysis of your data, followed by presentation of the analyzed (converted) data in a figure (graph), in a table, or in text.

Points to Consider When Writing the Results Section

- Do not discuss or interpret your results, report background information, or attempt to explain the analysis.
- Never include raw data or calculations in a research paper.
- Do not present the same data more than once.

- Text should complement any figures or tables, not repeat the same information.
- Do not confuse figures with tables. Figures include graphs, photographs, illustrations, diagrams, and so on. Tables have a row-and-column structure—that is, tables contain cells.

Discussion and Recommendations

The objective here is to provide an interpretation of your results and support for all your conclusions, using evidence from your survey results and generally accepted knowledge, if appropriate. The significance of findings should be clearly described.

Interpret your data in the discussion *in appropriate depth*. This means that when you explain a phenomenon, you must describe mechanisms that may account for the observation. If your results differ from your expectations, explain why that may have happened. If your results agree, then describe the theory that the evidence supported. It is never appropriate to simply state that the data agreed with expectations and let it drop at that.

- Decide if each hypothesis is supported or rejected, or if you cannot make a decision with confidence. Do not simply dismiss a study or a part of a study as "inconclusive."
- Research papers are not accepted if the work is incomplete. Draw what conclusions you can based on the results that you have, and identify the questions that remain unanswered and why.
- You may suggest future directions, such as how the survey might be modified to accomplish another objective.
- Explain all your observations as much as possible.
- Decide if the research design adequately addressed the hypothesis and whether or not it was properly controlled.
- Try to offer alternative explanations if reasonable alternatives exist.
- One survey research project will not answer all questions, so keeping the big picture in mind, where do you go next? The best studies open up new avenues of research. What questions remain? What recommendations do you have for future research?

References

List all the literature cited in your paper using the format dictated by the preferred style manual of the organization for which you are writing.

Appendix

This is where you include any pertinent information or copies of documents that do not fit within the body of the report. You may include materials such as a printed copy of the e-mail or Web questionnaire; the e-mail invitation; the consent form, if applicable; or detailed participant demographic data.

Oral Presentations

Oral presentations are another way of disseminating your survey results. Before you consider giving your presentation, you need to decide who your target audience is and be sure that the meeting or conference attendees will be interested in the topic of your survey. When you have a match between your topic and the audience, you can begin the preparation. It is useful to research specific information about the audience, such as their level of education and knowledge about the topic.

Preparing for Your Presentation

The presentation consists of three parts: the introduction, the main message, and the conclusion. Only 25% of your presentation should be dedicated to the introduction and the conclusion. The introduction defines the purpose of the presentation and the topics to be covered and captures the audience's interest. The main message section includes information about why the survey was conducted, how it was conducted, and the results. The conclusion influences the audience's ability to retain information and is, therefore, a crucial component of the presentation. The conclusion should not add any new information but should serve as a review of the major points of the presentation.

Designing Visual Aids

Visual aids have multiple benefits in an oral presentation if they are created correctly. Use visual aids to simplify complex ideas or concepts, share numeric data, help the audience organize ideas and understand abstractions, control the listeners' attention, and assist them with retaining the information. You can use visual aids to present a problem; show solutions and benefits; and illustrate processes, procedures, and steps in a sequence.

Common visual aids include a blackboard, a whiteboard, overhead slides, videotape, PowerPoint presentations, and handouts. PowerPoint shows are now the norm for academic and commercial presentations, and sometimes the copies of the slides are distributed as handouts; this is a handy way for audience members to follow the presentation and also a convenient way for them to take notes.

Transparencies and PowerPoint slides have pros and cons. Transparencies can be quickly prepared, are economical, and are easily carried and stored. The drawbacks are that projectors are bulky and may block the audience's view, and the process of changing from one transparency to another can be cumbersome. PowerPoint shows are easily stored and transported via portable media such as compact disks (CDs) or flash drives; are suitable for any size audience; can include colorful text, backgrounds, and graphics; and look professional. A downside of using PowerPoint is the reliance on technology; some sites may not have appropriate computers available. Of course, you can always take your own laptop computer, but this option cuts down on the convenience and portability of the PowerPoint show. Even if there are reliable computers in the presentation facility, it is still wise to include the PowerPoint Viewer on the disk or CD that contains your presentation. The PowerPoint Viewer allows users to present PowerPoint shows on computers that do not have PowerPoint software and is available for free downloading from the Microsoft Web site. A printed copy of the presentation is also a good idea as a final backup should all the technology fail.

Preparing PowerPoint Slides

PowerPoint slides serve as an outline for the speaker while helping the listeners to follow the presentation. PowerPoint is a software program that provides many options—that is, sounds, animation, transition effects, and so on. Be sure not to overuse animated graphics as they can become a source of distraction or, worse, annoyance to your audience.

An increasing number of Web survey hosts offer the ability to save figures and tables created on the site as PowerPoint (or MS Word) files. This "save as" feature can usually be found as an option located in the download menu of the survey software programs. Another option is to insert a hyperlink to the Web page containing your survey on one of the PowerPoint slides. This is an effective addition as the audience can view the questionnaire the same way the respondents did. Before doing this, however, it is imperative that you inquire about the Internet connectivity in the room where the presentation will be given. If the Internet connection in the facility is unreliable, it is advisable to insert pictures of the questionnaire pages (as .jpg or .pdf files) into your PowerPoint presentation rather than risk stalling the presentation while the computer searches for the Internet connection.

Below are some guidelines for creating and using PowerPoint slides:

- Allow approximately 1 to 2 minutes per slide.
- Each slide should have a title to orient the audience to the concept being presented.

- Limit each slide to one main concept.
- Use both uppercase and lowercase letters for each point to increase readability.
- All-uppercase letters should be used for the title only.
- Use a bullet before each point presented.
- Use phrases, not complete sentences.
- Use a maximum of nine lines per slide and six to eight words per line.
- Use dark backgrounds and light text.
- Do not overdo "cute" cartoons, complicated graphics, or elaborate backgrounds.
- Emphasize text with color, italics, and bold; do not underline words.
- Cite your sources and adhere to copyright laws.
- Use only two different types of fonts per slide (i.e., one for the title and one for the body).
- Use a maximum of three different sizes of font per slide.
- Exercise caution in using fonts with serifs—letters may appear to run together (e.g., Times New Roman).
- Font size should be about 20 point, but be careful as some fonts are smaller than others (Gouveia-Pisano, n.d.).

Examples of PowerPoint slides can be found in Figures 8.1 and 8.2.

Delivering Your Presentation

Delivering the presentation will call into action your basic public-speaking skills. An extensive discussion of the principles of public speaking is not appropriate here; however, we do provide a review of some of the factors worth noting as you contemplate delivering your presentation.

Dress Appropriately

Professional presentations require professional dress; usually, this means dressing in a fashion appropriate to the setting and consistent with the other presenters (if there are other presenters). Err on the side of overdressing if there is any doubt about what is suitable.

Be Aware of Nonverbal Communication

It is estimated that 55% of what the audience "hears" is gathered from nonverbal communications. This includes facial expressions, gestures, posture, and use of space. Strive to project a confident but natural style. Overuse of hand gestures to emphasize a point, for example, can be distracting and can lead to misunderstanding of the message.

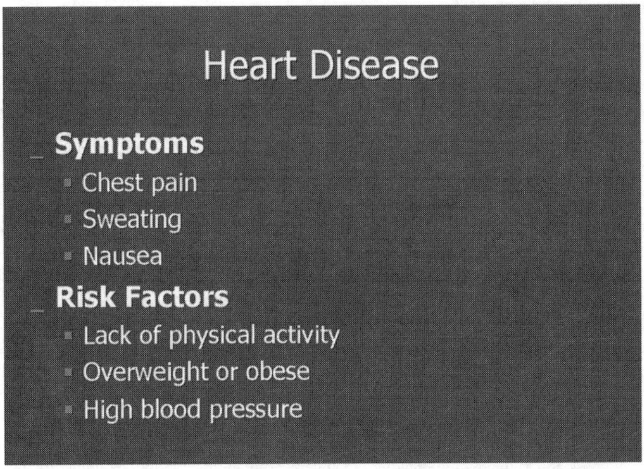

(a) Poor

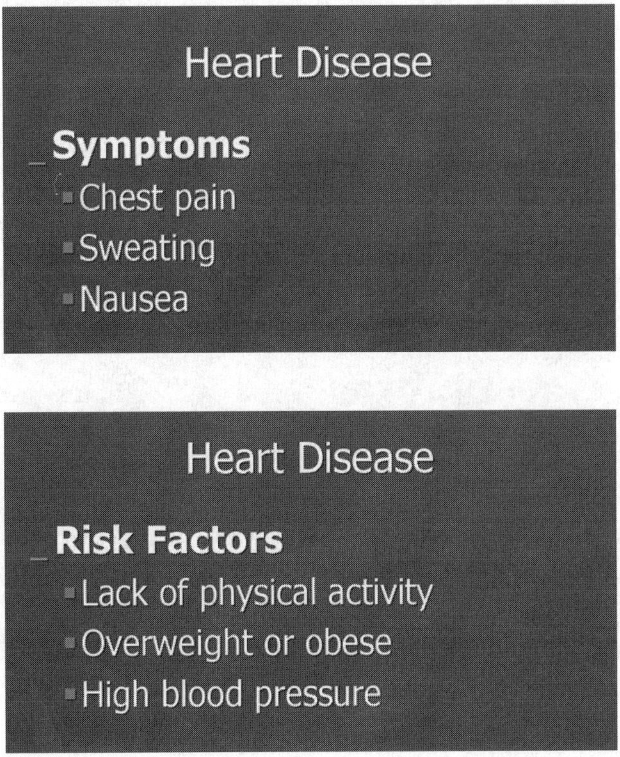

(b) Better

Figure 8.1 Example of a PowerPoint Slide

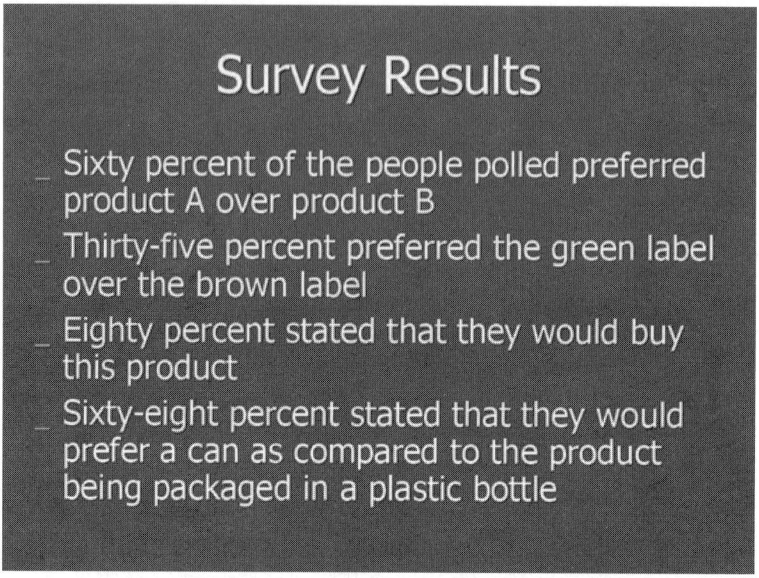

(a) Poor

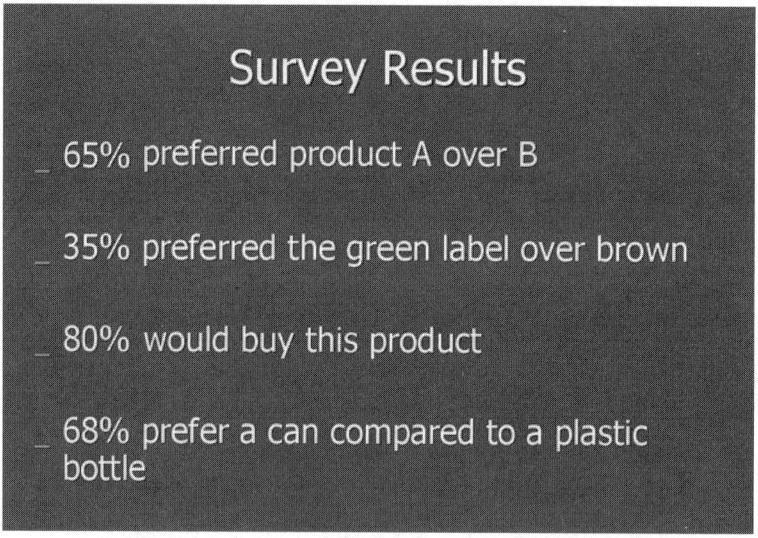

(b) Better

Figure 8.2   Another Example of a PowerPoint Slide

Manage Eye Contact

Eye contact with members of the audience is one of the most important aspects of effective message delivery. Speakers who are able to make appropriate eye contact with individual audience members are usually regarded as confident and trustworthy. Depending on the size of your audience, you will need to adjust the amount of eye contact you make with particular individuals. It is generally easier to maintain eye contact when audiences are large (at least it is easier to give the appearance of maintaining eye contact) than when they are small. In settings with small audiences, guard against gazing too long or too intently at individual audience members as this might be misinterpreted as hostility or a sexual overture.

Speak Slowly, Clearly, and Loudly

Use pitch, volume, and rate changes, including pauses, to add variety to your speech. Remind yourself to stress important words by highlighting key words or phrases in your notes.

Rehearse

Some experts recommend three rehearsals for formal presentations: one in front of your computer, especially important if you'll be demonstrating technical aspects of your online survey; another in front of a group of colleagues; and the third in the room where the presentation will take place (if possible). If extensive rehearsals are not feasible, try to go through your presentation at least once, making sure to time yourself so that you stay within the allotted time frame.

Poster Session Presentations

Poster exhibits are a popular way to present information about research projects at conferences. A benefit of poster presentations is the high level of conversation and personal interaction that authors and viewers can share. Also, posters can be displayed without the author being present. Individuals who are uncomfortable with giving presentations find posters to be a comfortable way of sharing their survey results.

The typical poster exhibit is an opportunity to visually display research and to illustrate investigations and findings. Projects are generally placed in a display area, and guests come and go as their schedules permit. Exhibitors stand by their work and are prepared to discuss their research with guests from all types of backgrounds.

A good poster will

1. draw attention to itself;

2. present information concisely, clearly, and completely; and

3. encourage questions and interchange with the author.

Preparing a Poster Exhibit

The content of your poster presentation is similar to that of the written report. You may include an abstract, background information, the purpose of the survey research project, information about the e-mail or Web survey, results, conclusions, and implications. While the content is similar, the presentation is significantly different: A poster is designed to highlight the major elements of the survey project and be viewed unaided, quickly, and usually from a distance.

Because people will be reviewing your presentation and not reading a paper, you will want to break information down into chunks or bite-sized pieces and use bulleted text when possible and appropriate. Do not simply paste your paper onto a poster board and call it a day. While a PowerPoint show previously created for an oral presentation may serve as a basis for a poster, it is unwise to print the pages of the PowerPoint show and paste them onto the poster board. PowerPoint slides created for an oral presentation will likely contain elements that require elaboration by the researcher and are not typically suitable for this presentation format.

The poster can be supplemented with a laptop computer on which the researcher can demonstrate the online survey, provided that the exhibit space is adequately equipped. If wired (or wireless) Internet connections are not available, it is still possible to demonstrate the questionnaire on a laptop; the survey won't be "live," that is, viewers can't fill in answers, but they will be able to view static images of pages of the questionnaire.

Appearance of Your Poster

Your poster should be professional and attractive. The goal is to make it as visually appealing as possible without being cluttered. Sizes of posters vary widely; you should inquire about your space allocation if the information is not readily available. Aim to create a poster that will fill the available space without being overwhelming. As a guideline, a typical display panel is about 36 inches high by 23 inches wide. A photo of a sample poster can be found in Figure 8.3. The following are some specific recommendations for constructing posters for the presentation of research results.

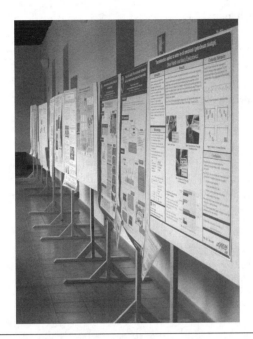

Figure 8.3   Photo of a Poster Presentation

Text

Limit text to a maximum of 15 lines per page and avoid abbreviations, acronyms, and jargon. Bulleted lists help readers break down information into digestible bits; limit bullets to between five and seven per sheet. Each bullet should focus on one point and be no longer than a sentence or two. Use upper- and lowercase type in a font size that is large enough to be read from a distance of about 3 feet. (See Table 8.1 for guidelines regarding font sizes for poster exhibits.)

Graphs and Photographs

Include graphs or photographs in place of text whenever possible. Ensure that the graphs you choose are directly related to the text and are fully explained in a caption or legend. As with text, illustrative material should be

Table 8.1   Typical Type Sizes for Exhibits

Heading	Font size
Logo, headers	5½ inches (reverse type is effective)
First headline—main panel	120 point
Second headline or large bullet items	72 point
Smaller bullet items	48–60 point
Text blocks	30–36 point
Captions	18–24 point

SOURCE: © Copyright 2006 Los Alamos National Security.

clearly visible from a distance of about 3 feet; the lettering on illustrations should be at least 3/8 inch high. Consider the viewers' cone of vision (see Figure 8.4) when assembling the elements of the poster.

Color

Use color liberally to emphasize titles, graphs, and photos. However, be wary of using too many different colors on one poster as this may lend a childlike appearance to the product. Individual pages and photos can be mounted on colored poster board panels that complement the colors in the poster. Textured papers and mats also may be attractive additions, so long as the text is still legible, especially in rooms with dim lighting.

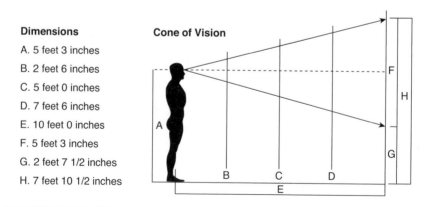

Dimensions

A. 5 feet 3 inches
B. 2 feet 6 inches
C. 5 feet 0 inches
D. 7 feet 6 inches
E. 10 feet 0 inches
F. 5 feet 3 inches
G. 2 feet 7 1/2 inches
H. 7 feet 10 1/2 inches

Cone of Vision

Figure 8.4   Cone of Vision

SOURCE: © Copyright 2006 Los Alamos National Security.

Organization

Each of the panels on the poster should be numbered to guide the viewer through the poster; number the panels and arrange them to read from left to right rather than from top to bottom. A brief, one-page handout containing the main points on the poster, the URL of the survey, and perhaps the survey results. The researcher's contact information is also a useful addition to a poster session presentation.

Visual Aids

Whether you are writing a report or giving an oral presentation, visual aids can help your audience understand the results. Visuals assist in comprehending the information and in making numbers easier to grasp and compare. Below is a list of the benefits of using graphics:

1. Graphics make concepts easier to understand.

2. Color, fonts, and graphics can help the reader comprehend an idea.

3. Graphics support and emphasize ideas.

4. Graphics generate interest and attract attention.

5. Graphics are important and powerful when integrated with text.

Basic Web survey hosts have the ability to create graphics (such as histograms or pie charts) in their reporting feature. These graphs, however, are not usually easy to export for use in a report or oral presentation. As noted previously, some hosts are beginning to offer an upgrade (for an additional fee) that allows users to directly export graphs as MS Word or PowerPoint files. If this feature is not available in the program that you are using, you will be able to export your data as an Excel file and from there create the charts and graphs you need. (*Note:* It is advisable to sign up for a Web survey host that allows you to export your raw data as an Excel file.)

General Guidelines for Creating Graphics

To communicate information effectively in graphs, each one should have a clear purpose, usually to illustrate a point made in the text. Verify that the data contained in your charts or figures are correct and that the format is simple and uncluttered. Graphs should be comprehensible on their own but should relate to something in the text. There are many different ways to display your data in graphic format; it is important to choose the graph that is most appropriate for the type of data you are presenting. Below are different types of graphs and diagrams that you can use and some guidelines on how to effectively use the tools.

Pie Charts

Pie charts show relationships among the elements that comprise a whole. They should be used only when you are describing 100% of something. For example, all the responses to a particular survey question or all the age groups of the sample population are appropriate for pie charts. An important consideration when creating pie charts is the scale. Each part must be in proportion to the percentage that it represents. Limit pie "slices" to not more than six or seven or it will look too cluttered. Label your pie chart clearly either by using a legend or by using words on the graph, as in the example in Figure 8.5. If you have six or seven slices, you should use a legend so that the text is legible.

If you are surveying nonprofit agencies to see how their money is spent, you may end up with a pie chart like the one in Figure 8.5.

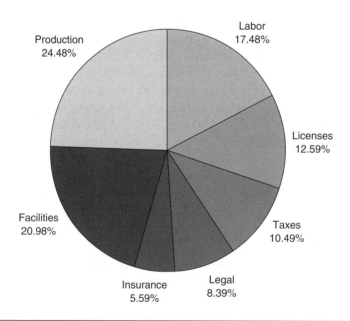

Figure 8.5   Example of a Pie Chart

Bar Graphs

Bar graphs are an effective way to display survey data because they provide an overview of a variety of types of data at a quick glance. Bar graphs should be used to display data at one point in time. Bar graphs can be displayed vertically (see Figure 8.6) or horizontally (see Figure 8.7).

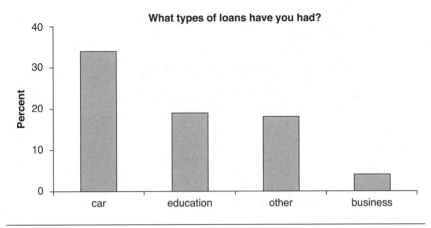

Figure 8.6   Example of a Vertical Bar Chart

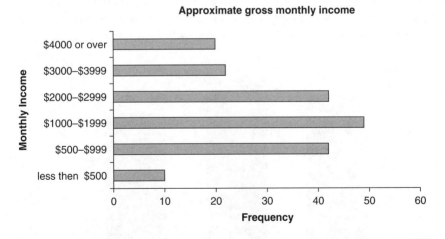

Figure 8.7   Example of a Horizontal Bar Chart

You also can use bar graphs to effectively compare information by grouping data. For example, you may want to compare the survey responses for males and females or to compare responses at different work sites. The example in Figure 8.8 shows how bar graphs can be used to compare groups or show changes.

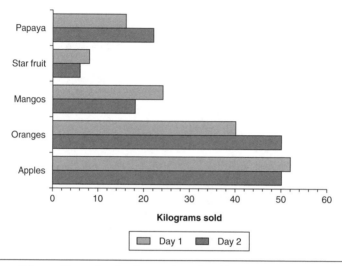

Figure 8.8   Example of a Comparison Bar Chart

Stacked bar graphs show groups of data together. Stacked bars display all the values in a category as one bar, with each separate value color coded on the bar according to the series it came from. As with pie charts, stacked bar graphs should be used only when you are describing 100% of something. An example of a stacked bar graph can be found in Figure 8.9.

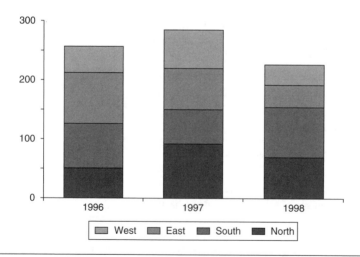

Figure 8.9   Example of a Stacked Bar Graph

Line Graphs

Line graphs can compare groups or show changes over time. Like bar graphs, the developer must be responsible and not make a variable look significantly different from another by overemphasizing the change using the scale. In Figure 8.10, there is an example of a line graph.

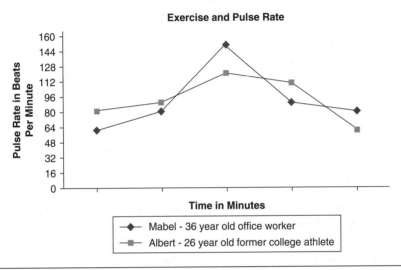

Figure 8.10   Example of a Line Graph

Venn Diagrams

A Venn diagram is an illustration of the relationships between groups that share something in common. Usually, Venn diagrams are used to depict set intersections (denoted by the upside-down letter U). Figure 8.11 is an example of a Venn diagram that shows the relationship among three overlapping sets A, B, and C. An example of how this would be applied to survey research is that a researcher may survey high school students and want to illustrate how many of them, within the previous 3 months, have smoked cigarettes, drank alcohol, or smoked cigarettes and drank alcohol.

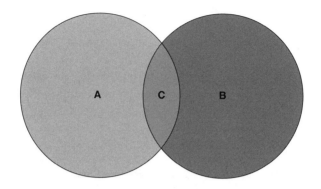

Legend
A = Students who smoked cigarettes within the last three months
B = Students who drank alcohol within the last three months
C = Students who smokes cigarettes and drank alcohol within the last three months

Figure 8.11   Example of a Venn Diagram

Flowcharts

Flowcharts are diagrams that provide a visual image of a project or process. These diagrams can be very helpful in explaining a process. They are especially useful to describe the process by which your study was conducted. Usually, the shape of the box in the flowchart is representative of a type of step in the process. For example, an arrow usually indicates movement, a diamond may indicate a decision, a square may indicate a process or action, and a line often indicates the flow of the system from one process or decision to another. You should be consistent in how you use the symbols. Figure 8.12 on the next page shows an example of a flowchart.

Scatter Plots

A scatter plot or scatter graph is a graph used to visually display and compare two or more sets of related quantitative or numerical data. The scatter plot enables the reader to obtain a visual comparison of the two sets of data and help determine what kind of relationship there might be between them. Each data point has a coordinate on a horizontal and a vertical axis. A dot in the body of the chart represents the intersection of the data on the x and y axes.

Scatter plots should be used when showing relationships between variables and display the direction of the relationship (positive or negative). These graphs also show the strength of the relationship.

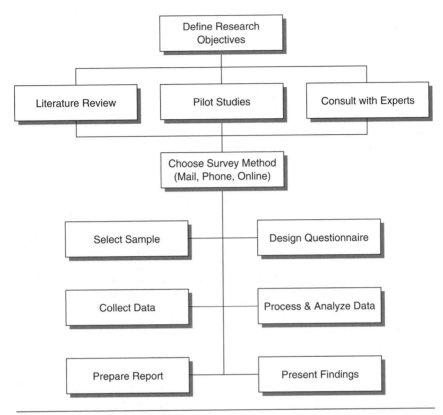

Figure 8.12   Example of a Flowchart of the Research Process

Box Plots

The box plot also is called a box-and-whiskers plot. Though it looks very different from the previous graphs, it is an effective way to show survey results. To create a box-and-whisker plot, draw a box with ends at the quartiles Q_1 and Q_3. Draw the statistical median M as a horizontal line in the box. Next, extend the "whiskers" to the farthest points that are not outliers (outliers are within 3/2 times the interquartile range of Q_1 and Q_3). Then, for every point more than 3/2 times the interquartile range from the end of the box, draw a dot. If two dots have the same value, draw them side by side (Wolfram Research, n.d.). The box (the rectangular portion of the graph) extends from Q_1 to Q_3, with a horizontal line segment indicating the median. Figure 8.14 shows the construction of a box plot, and Figure 8.15 is an example of a box plot.

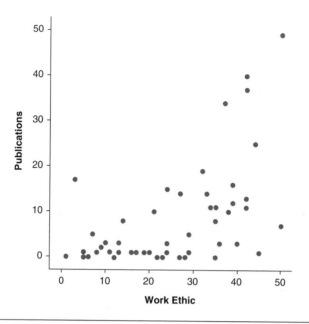

Figure 8.13   Example of a Scatter Plot

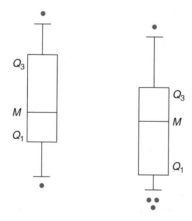

Figure 8.14   Example of the Construction of a Box Plot

Stem-and-Leaf Display

A stem-and-leaf display, also called a stem-and-leaf plot, is a diagram that quickly summarizes data while maintaining the individual data points. In such a diagram, the "stem" is a column of the unique elements of data

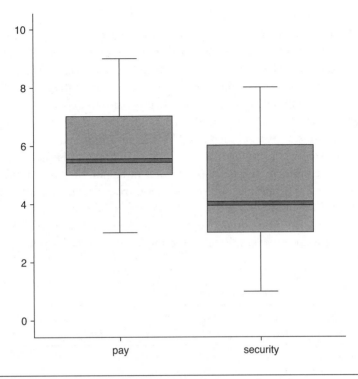

Figure 8.15   Example of a Box Plot

after removing the last digit. The final digits ("leaves") of each column are then placed in a row next to the appropriate column and sorted in numerical order.

Table 8.2 shows the stem-and-leaf diagram for the data set (147, 117, 101, 149, 145, 105, 93, 94, 114, 104, 136, 140, 121, 145, 120, 142, 98, 135, 135, 132).

Table 8.2   Example of a Stem-and-Leaf Display

Stem	Leaves
9	3, 4, 8
10	1, 4, 5
11	4, 7
12	0, 1
13	2, 5, 5, 6
14	0, 2, 5, 5, 7, 9

Tables

Tables have rows and columns and enable you to show your data in an easy-to-read format. Tables are only necessary for large amounts of data that would be too complicated to present in the text. If you need to present a few numbers, you should do so directly in the text, not in a table.

The table should make sense on its own. Be sure to explain all abbreviations except standard abbreviations such as *M, SD,* and *df.* Do not forget to identify the units of measurement, and list the information in a logical order. The order usually is from most to least frequent. Do not discuss every piece of data in the table, or else there is no point in having the table. Only mention the most important pieces of information from the table. Tables should appear within the paper or in the appendix. Every table needs a unique title after its label. The title should be brief but clearly explain what is in the table. Table 8.3 is an example of a descriptive table in APA format.

Table 8.3   Sample Descriptive Table in APA Format

Statements	Strongly Agree (%)	Agree (%)	Disagree (%)	Strongly Disagree %	Total (%)
Satisfaction	42	47	11	0	100
Perception	38	49	10	3	100

Another way to present the survey results is to include the survey questions and list the results next to them. Table 8.4 provides an example of this approach.

Table 8.4   Example of a Table for a Specific Survey Question

Question 10: "How satisfied were you with the service at this facility?"	Response to Question 10 (%)	
	Female Customers (N = 80)	Male Customers (N = 30)
Very satisfied	22	17
Satisfied	27	17
Unsatisfied	34	40
Very unsatisfied	16	27

Matching Survey Results to Type of Display

In many situations, you will have a choice about the type of tables and graphs to represent your data; other circumstances will demand a particular table or chart. As mentioned previously, pie charts should be used only when describing the percentage each part of a whole occupies, whereas line graphs are appropriate for showing changes over time. Table 8.5 provides examples of how a circumstance may be matched with a graphic or table that will best illustrate it.

Table 8.5   Examples of How Graphics and Tables Can Be Used to Represent Data

Survey Results	Display Type
1. A comparison of voting behaviors of people in three counties	Table
2. How people spend their time	Pie chart
3. Changes in survey participants' reported pain levels over time	Line chart
4. Satisfaction levels of four departments in a work site	Bar chart
5. Demographic information of survey participants	Table
6. No. of survey participants who drink Coca Cola, Pepsi, or both	Venn diagram
7. Education levels of survey participants	Pie chart
8. The ages of the people who responded to the survey	Stem and leaf display
9. Comparison of reported levels of depression of males and females	Box plot
10. The relationship of reported stress levels and time spent exercising	Scatter Plot

Distributing Results Using a Web-Based Survey Development Tool

Most of the Web-based survey development tools will allow users to share survey results created by the Web site. This is an easy way to share simple descriptive data with colleagues or respondents. The reports can contain colorful tables and graphs that are automatically created by the Web program. Many survey hosts are limited to simple tables, bar graphs, and pie charts. If you would like to share more advanced results or a different variety of graphs, you will need to first export the data (either in raw form or as summary statistics) and compute the analyses or create the graphs in another program. Appendix G shows an example of a basic SurveyMonkey results report.

There are usually a few options for sharing the results. Zoomerang, for example, allows users to share results in a "restricted" mode, where only summary statistics can be viewed by others but individual responses can be viewed by the survey owner, and a "public" mode, where summary and individual results can be viewed by others.

Dissemination options include placing the URL link to the report on a Web page or including the URL in an e-mail message. For example, the URL of the report page might be included in a "thank-you" e-mail message so that respondents can view the results.

Summary

After doing the work of obtaining the survey results, you have the opportunity to share your findings in an oral or written format or both. Reporting your findings is as valuable as conducting the survey research, because sharing what you have learned is an important part of increasing the knowledge base of your field. In this chapter, we have covered the various modes of information dissemination: written reports, oral presentations, poster exhibits, and electronic distribution. Researchers typically use more than one method to share the information they have collected. While the information remains the same no matter how you choose to report it, it is important to tailor the form of the report to fit the manner of presentation by adhering to the general principles of written, oral, visual, and electronic modes of communication.

9

Concluding Comments

The field of online survey research is young and rapidly developing. Some experts predict that online, particularly Web-based, surveys will eventually replace other modes of survey administration. We believe that online surveys will continue to evolve and eventually take their place amid the collection of methodological options as a unique response mode ideally suited to certain situations.

In this chapter, we recap some of the important considerations surrounding the use of online surveys; reexamine the benefits associated with their use—namely that online surveys are faster, cheaper, and sometimes more effective than other methods; and offer some concluding thoughts about the future of online survey research.

Opportunities and Challenges in Online Survey Research

We began this text by presenting a list of factors for researchers to ponder when deciding on a survey research mode. Having discussed in detail each of the important considerations, we now offer the following summary: Online surveys are an effective mode of survey administration when dealing with closed populations, when probability sampling is not essential, and when the target respondents have access to the necessary computer technology.

Closed populations provide the optimal situation for the use of online surveys. They typically have existing sampling frames such as e-mail lists of employees, members, or students; potential respondents will be familiar with the organization and may regard the survey as official business; and the subject matter is likely to be of interest and relevance to the respondents. For example, a global aerospace company that seeks to collect information about safety procedures from their internationally distributed group of engineers can easily send an e-mail message to the employees inviting them to link to a Web page containing the safety questionnaire. The employees will be motivated to participate in the survey because it is generated by their employer and the subject matter is pertinent to their jobs.

The current developmental state of online surveys does not allow for easy probability sampling of respondents from open populations. This significantly limits the use of Internet-based surveys when the research goal is to make inferences about larger populations. Presently, the most successful use of probability sampling in online surveys involves a mixed-mode design wherein respondents are first contacted by telephone or postal mail and then directed to a Web site to complete the questionnaire. While there is some marginal time saving because the data entry chore is eliminated, it is not clear whether this technique increases response rate in any noticeable way. It is, therefore, best to employ online surveys of general populations when convenience sampling will suffice, such as in the case of pilot studies.

Although household penetration of Internet technology continues to increase, it is not yet pervasive; furthermore, the distribution of those who have adopted the technology is concentrated among people under 65 years of age, the college educated, and people with higher than average household incomes. Technological barriers, such as spam filters, pop-up blockers, and spyware, which are designed to protect privacy and ensure online security, also present challenges for online survey researchers. People can easily block uninvited e-mails and stop e-mail invitations from arriving in their in-box. Lack of computer literacy and physical disabilities also prevent access to online surveys in some target populations. Technological advancements are being made to improve access for everyone, but there is still a need for further expansion.

Benefits of Online Surveys

Online survey research offers the promise of speed, economy, and improved data quality. As we have discussed in the preceding chapters, and summarize here, these benefits hold only in limited circumstances. Web surveys are faster than traditional methods when respondents are contacted via e-mail and directed to a Web host to complete the questionnaire. In this situation, there is the potential for researchers to create and field the survey and be ready for data analysis in a matter of days.

Online surveys are relatively inexpensive to conduct. The researcher saves on printing, mail, interviewer, and data entry costs. Although software, Web hosting, and staff time to develop the online questionnaire are necessary expenditures, there is a variety of low-cost software and Web-hosting options on the market that feature simple user interfaces and are designed for novice online survey researchers. For research projects aimed at surveying large numbers of geographically dispersed individuals, online surveys offer an affordable option.

Although significant challenges related to coverage area and response rates remain, there are some applications in which online surveys are superior to other methods. Online surveys are well suited to situations where interviewer bias or a tendency toward providing socially desirable answers may threaten the validity of the data. Similarly, if a questionnaire contains numerous open-ended questions, emerging evidence indicates that respondents provide longer, and often more valid, answers in online surveys than on paper questionnaires. Moreover, skip patterns and interactive tasks can be effectively used online.

The Future of Online Survey Research

A considerable body of literature surrounding online survey research is developing. Researchers working in this area face a variety of intriguing questions about the best use of online surveys, such as the following: What is the optimal questionnaire design? What is the most effective use of incentives in Web and e-mail surveys? How can sampling frames of open populations be generated? How can pre-recruited panels of respondents be most successfully used? How should data collected from phone or postal mail surveys be combined with data collected from online surveys? These questions, along with techniques for increasing response rates and distinguishing research surveys from the profusion of entertainment surveys on the Web, will surely occupy the attention of survey research scholars.

It is impossible to predict all the technological and cultural changes that will confront survey researchers in the coming years; it is safe to say, however, that online survey research is here to stay. As computer technology advances and the Internet becomes more diffused in society and more integrated into individuals' daily lives, there will be new challenges and opportunities for methodologists. It is our hope that this volume will serve as a useful guide for those who seek to answer research questions using online survey research.

Appendix A

Resource Guide

Online Statistics Books

Name of Book	Author	Web Site
SURFSTAT	Keith Dear	www.anu.edu.au/nceph/surfstat/surfstat home/surfstat.html
SticiGui	P. B. Stark	www.stat.berkeley.edu/~stark/SticiGui/ index.htm
Statistics at Square One	T D V Swinscow	http://bmj.bmjjournals.com/collections/ statsbk/index.shtml
Concepts and Applications of Inferential Statistics	Robert Lowry	http://vassun.vassar.edu/~lowry/webtext .html
Introductory Statistics: Concepts, Models, and Applications	David W. Stockburger	www.psychstat.missouristate.edu/sbk00 .htm
Multivariate Statistics	David W. Stockburger	www.psychstat.missouristate.edu/multi book/mlt00.htm
A New View of Statistics	Will Hopkins	www.sportsci.org/resource/stats/index .html
Introduction to Data Collection and Analysis	Albert Goodman	www.deakin.edu.au/~agoodman/sci101/ index.php
Statnotes: An Online Textbook	G. David Garson	www2.chass.ncsu.edu/garson/pa765/ statnote.htm

Online Survey Software and Web Survey Hosts

Product	Company	Web Site
2ask	Amundis Communications	www.2ask.de/
Absolute poll manager	XIGLA SOFTWARE	www.xigla.com/absolutepm/index
ActionPoll	Open Source Technology Group	http://sourceforge.net/projects/action
Adenquire.net	Andreas Schroeder	www.adenquire.net/br/index.php
Advanced Survey	iSixSigma	www.advancedsurvey.com/surveys/
Amae CI Suite	Amae Software	www.amaesoftware.com
Anonymous-feedback	Anonymous-Feedback	www.anonymous-feedback.com
AppForce.net	MarketProven	www.appforce.net
Applynet Survey	Eastisoft	www.applynet.net
ask4more	www.ask4more.biz	http://ask4more.biz
AskAnywhere	Senecio Software	www.senecio.com/askanywhere.html
Askia Design—with Askia Web	Askia	www.askia.com
BallotBin	BallotBin	www.ballotbin.com
Beeliner online survey software	Spinfish Web/ROG	www.beelinersurveys.com
Bellview Web	Pulse Train Software	www.pulsetrain.com/solutions
Blaise	Statistics Netherlands	www.cbs.nl/en-GB/menu
Blue/360	eXplorance	www.explorance.com
Campus-Vote	Campus-Vote	www.campus-vote.com
CheckMarket Online Surveys	CheckMarket Corporation	www.checkmarket.com/fe/products
CleverForm ASP	CleverForm	www.cleverform.com

(Continued)

(Continued)

Product	Company	Web Site
ClickSurvey	ClickSurvey	www.clicksurvey.com
ClientSurveys.ca	ClientSurveys.ca	www.clientsurveys.ca
CockpitSurvey	4GHI	www.4ghi.com
Confirmit	FIRM-Future Information Research Management	www.confirmit.com
Cont@xt	Information Factory	www.information-factory.com
ConveneMachine Survey Tools	ConveneMachine	www.convenemachine.com
Cool Surveys	Majon International	www.coolsurveys.com
CRM Q+	CRM Survey Inc.	www.crmsurvey.com
CustomerSat Enterprise	CustomerSat	www.customersat.com
CustomInsight	CustomInsight	www.custominsight.com
Custom Web Surveys	CustomWeb Surveys	www.customwebsurveys.com
DAP diRec	DAP-Software-Büro GmbH	www.dap-software.de
DASH	DASH Software	www.dash.ca/
Data Blocks Magenta Suite	SurveySystems	www.sur-sys.com
Datacurious	Datacurious	www.datacurious.com
Demographix	Demographix	www.demographix.com
Digipop Web Surveys	Digipop	www.digipop.com
Dragon Web Surveys 6.5	oAzium-Waves in Motion	www.wmotion.com
Dub InterViewer	Nebu bv	www.nebu.com
DynaSurv	TreeLogic	www.treelogic-swe.com
e-Questionnaire	HyperObjects	www.e-questionnaire.com
Easy Survey	MAPILab	www.mapilab.com

Product	Company	Web Site
Easyquizz 2005	Epistema	www.epistema.com
Easyresearch	Ciceronex AB	www.easyresearch.se/survey/
echopoll.com	Preyer Information Technology	http://echopoll.com
EForm	Beach Tech	www.beachtech.com
Electronic Survey Manager	Case Sensitive Solutions	www.casesensitive.com.au/prod/ esm.php
eListen 2005	Scantron Corporation	www.scantron.com/siteSpecific/
EMail Response Application (ERA)	Pilodata	www.pilodata.de/era/index.jsp
Enalyzer Survey Solution 5.2	Enalyzer	www.enalyzer.com
EnnectSurvey	Elliance	www.ennect.com
enterraVOTE	Enterra	www.enterravote.de
eQ	TeleSage	www.telesage.com/eQ.html
eQuestionnaire	Paul Marx-Marketing Consulting	http://home.equestionnaire.de
Equip	ISI GmbH	www.equip-software.de
eRes	Fakultät für Psychologie der Universität Basel	http://webserver.psycho.unibas.ch
ESP—Electronic Survey Program	Gepeto Software	www.gepetosoftware.com/esp.htm
eSurvey	Help Desk Software Solution	www.parature.com/esurvey.aspx
eSurvey	Corporate Renaissance Group	www.crgroup.com
Exam	Envel Informationssyst eme GmbH	www.myexam.net
Exavo SurveyStudio	Exavo	http://exavo.de/online-umfrage software-internet-befragung software.htm

(Continued)

(Continued)

Product	Company	Web Site
EZSurvey	Raosoft	www.raosoft.com
FatCast Online Survey	FatCast.com	www.fatcast.com
FeedbackToday	FeedbackToday	www.feedbacktoday.com
FormArtist	Quask	www.quask.com/en/products.asp
FormGuide	Gölz & Schwarz	www.goelz.com
Free Online Surveys	Problem Free	www.free-online-surveys.co.uk
Free Polls	United Online	www.freepolls.com
Freesurveysonline.com	MAP Business Solutions Inc.	www.freesurveysonline.com
getFAST	Mount Royal College	www.getfast.ca
Globalscape Websurvey	GlobalSCAPE	www.globalscape.com/websurvey
Grader	Fusion Software	www.fusionsoftware.co.uk
Grapevine	Grapevine	www.grapevinesurveys.com
Halogen eSurveyor	Halogen Software	www.halogensoftware.com
Hosted Survey 5	Hostedware Corporation	www.hostedsurveylite.com
i-replies.com	i-replies.com	www.i-replies.com/ireplies.asp
IB Quest	Inooga Solutions	www.inooga.com
iiON SmartSuite	iiON Corporation	http://corporate.iion.com
iMercury	Pulse Train Software	www.pulsetrainsw.com
iNetSurvey	iNetSurvey	www.inetsurvey.com
Infocounts	Infocounts	www.infocounts.com
Infoluchs X3	Geschäftsbereich KSID	www.umfragesoftware.de
Infopoll Web Survey Suite	Infopoll Incorporated	http://infopoll.com/live/surveys
Inquery	Inworks	www.inworks.de/inquery.html
Inquisite Web Survey System	Inquisite	www.inquisite.com

Product	Company	Web Site
InSite Survey System	InSite	www.insitesurveys.com
Insiteful Surveys	Insiteful Surveys	www.insitefulsurveys.com
InstantSurvey	NetReflector	www.netreflector.com
IntelliQuest	Millward Brown IntelliQuest	www.intelliquest.com
Interactive Survey Manager	Interactive Sales Solutions	www.issi-ivr.com
Internet Services	ZonderaCom AB	www.zondera.com
Internet Survey	Blizinski, Maciej	http://insuren.sourceforge.net
Internet Surveys	Macro International Inc.	www.orcmacro.com
Interviewer	Voxco	www.voxco.com
Interwiew?! 5.2	Interview SA	www.123interview.com
InViewsion	Global Reach Internet Productions	www.inviewsion.com
Ioxphere	Xorbix Technologies	www.ioxphere.com
IRQuest	Interrogare GmbH	www.interrogare.com
IT Web	Interview Technology	www.interviewtechnology.com
IYSS	The Gosling Group	www.d-q-e.com
J-Quest	jvp Datentechnik	www.j-quest.de
Jambo	Jambo Software	www.jambo-software.com
Keypoint	Logotron	www.camsp.com/index.php
KeySurvey	Key Survey	www.keysurvey.com
KMailer	Brezosoft Inc.	www.kmailer.com
LearningBridge	LearningBridge	www.learningbridge.com
LetMeKnow	LetMeKnow	www.letmeknow.ch/software
Lightning Survey	Tensor	www.lightningsurvey.com

(Continued)

(Continued)

Product	Company	Web Site
Lightspeed Panels	Lightspeed Research	www.lightspeedresearch.com
MafoMaker	Antwerpes & Partner AG	www.mafomaker.de/inhalt1.htm
MagnetMail	Real Magnet	www.realmagnet.com
MakeSurvey	Baltsoft	www.makesurvey.net
Marketing Survey Tool	Radoslav Kmiecick	www.surveyworld.org
MemDB Online Survey System	MemDB Technology Company	www.memdb.com
Mobile Memoir	Mobile Memoir	www.mobilememoir.com
MobileSurvey	Perseus Development Corporation	www.perseus.com
Mod_Survey	ITM	www.modsurvey.org
MojoPoll	TELA IT	www.mojoscripts.com
mrInterview	SPSS	www.spss.com
Multi-Platform Survey Architect	Open Source Technology Group	http://sourceforge.net
MyOnlineForms	Net-O	www.myonlineforms.com
NBsurvey	WesternConnect	http://netbrainbox.co.uk
Net Survey	Soft-Concept	http://ethnosoft.com
Net-MR Net-Survey	Global Market Insite	www.gmi-mr.com
NetQuestionnaires	NetQuestionnaires	www.netquestionnaires.de
NetTeam.Survey	NetTeam	www.nmsl.co.uk
NIPO Web Interview System	NIPO	www.nipo-software.com
ODTools Survey System	ODTools.com	www.odtools.com
OfficeSeries Internet Survey System	General Blue Corporation	www.officeseries.com

Product	Company	Web Site
Online Survey Creator	Solutech Systems	www.onlinesurveycreator.com
Online Survey Solution	M/A/R/C Research	www.marcresearch.com
Online survey tool	Ewwwtek	www.ewwwtek.com
Online Surveys	Web Online Surveys	http://web-online-surveys.com
Online Surveys	The Business Research Lab	www.busreslab.com
Online Surveys	Nooro Online Research	www.nooro.com
Online Surveys	Kinesis Survey Technologies	www.kinesissurvey.com
OnlineUmfragen.com	Pstar Group Ltd	www.onlineumfragen.com
Opinio	ObjectPlanet	www.objectplanet.com
Opinion Search Online Services	Opinion Search	www.opinionsearch.com
OpinionPort	SRBI	www.srbi.com
OpinionPower .com—Polls and Surveys	OpinionPower .com	www.opinionpower.com
Opquest	Opquest: A Division Of Opquest: A Division Of Business Solutions	http://opquest.com
Origin Survey Manager	Madgex Limited	www.madgex.com
Panel +	VisionCritical	www.visioncritical.com
PapayaPolls	Perceptus Solutions	www.papayapolls.com
Perception für das Web	Questionmark Europe	www.questionmark.com
Perennial Survey	Perennial Survey	www.perennialsurvey.com
phpESP	phpESP	http://phpesp.sourceforge.net

(Continued)

(Continued)

Product	Company	Web Site
phpQuestionnaire/ PerlQuestionnaire	Chumpsoft	www.chumpsoft.com
phpSurvey	phpSurvey	http://phpsurvey.sourceforge.net
phpSurveyor	phpSurveyor	www.phpsurveyor.org
Poll Pro	Expinion.net	www.expinion.net
Poll Pro 2.0	AdComplete	www.pollpro.com/default.asp
PollCat Surveys	PollCat	http://pollcat.com
Polls Pro	United Online	www.freepolls.com
PollStream	PollStream	www.pollstream.com
Populus Web-Based Survey	Populus	www.populus.com
Primal Egg Survey Application	Primal Egg Creations	www.collectdatanow.com
Print & Scan	Trax UK	www.trax-uk.co.uk
Pro-Quest	PRO QUEST	www.pro-quest.de
Procevo	Evolutia Design Ltd.	www.procevo.com
Pronto Survey	Bebosoft, Inc.	www.bebosoft.com
QEDML Designer	Philology	www.qedml.com.au
QGen	Dipro AG	www.quiz-gen.com
Qstation Survey	QStation	http://survey.qstation.com
Quality Benchmark	Ceram research	www.qualitybenchmark.com
Query&Report	Artisan Global Software	www.artologik.net
Query-Portal	Eplit GmbH	www.eplit.com
QuestionData 6	GrimmerSoft	www.grimmersoft.com
QuestionPro*	QuestionPro	www.questionpro.com
Quik-Poll	Silver Creek	www.touchbase.com
Quikpolls	Tuglet.com	www.quikpolls.com
Remark Web Survey 3	Gravic	www.principiaproducts.com
ResearchExec	ResearchExec	www.researchexec.com

Product	Company	Web Site
RformSurvey	my3q	www.rform.com
Ridgecrest Surveys	Ridgecrest Marketing	www.ridgecrestsurveys.com
rospV4	Gieler Marktforschungs-Software	www.online-survey.at
Rostock Survey Tool	Hinner, Kajetan	www.hinner.com
SelectSurveyASP	ClassApps	www.classapps.com
SENATE	BlueShift	www.blueshift.com
Sensorpro	Narragansett Technologies	www.narragansett.ie
Sensus Web	Sawtooth Technologies	www.sawtooth.com
SmartASK	WebSlingerZ	http://smartask.biz
SmartSurveys	mySmart Solutions, LC	www.smartsurveys.net
snap ProNet Edition	Mercator Research Group	www.snapsurveys.com
Socrates Questionnaire Engine	Open Source Technology Group	http://socrates-qe.sourceforge.net
Socratic Web Survey	Socratic Technologies	www.sotech.com
Software G3	Rogator Software	www.rogator.de
Software G4	Rogator Software	www.rogator.de
SpeedSurvey	SpeedSurvey	www.speedsurvey.com
Sphinx	Electric Paper	www.electricpaper.de
Sphinx-survey	sphinx-survey	www.sphinxdevelopment.co.uk
SSI Web	Sawtooth Software	www.sawtoothsoftware.com
SSI-SNAP Online Ordering System	Survey Sampling International	www.surveysampling.com
StateSurvey.com	Metro data	www.statesurvey.com
StatPac for Windows	StatPac	www.statpac.com

(Continued)

(Continued)

Product	Company	Web Site
StellarSurvey	StellarSurvey	www.stellarsurvey.com
STEPS Surveys	Cierant Corporation	www.cierant.com
Streaming Survey	SurveyWriter	www.streamingsurvey.com
SumQuest	SumQuest Survey Software	www.sumquest.com
SuperSurvey	Tercent	www.supersurvey.com
SurJey	Open Source Technology Group	http://surjey.sourceforge.net
Survaze	Survaze	www.survaze.com
Survey Box	YellowHawk Limited	www.yellowhawk.co.uk
Survey Builder	eBrands	www.surveybuilder.com.au
Survey Crafter	Survey Crafter	www.surveycrafter.com
Survey Galaxy	Survey Galaxy	www.surveygalaxy.com
Survey Genie Gold	William Steinberg Consultants	www.notjustsurveys.com
Survey Gold 7.0	Golden Hills Software	www.surveygold.com
Survey Hosting Service	Survey-Hosting.com	www.survey-hosting.com
Survey Internet	Aufrance Associates	http://aufrance.com/survey.htm
Survey Manager	Australian Survey Research	www.aussurveys.com
Survey Manager	Strategies	www.strategies.co.uk
Survey Manager v1.3-Encuestas Online	Netquest	www.netquest.es
Survey Power	WISCO Computing	www.wiscocomputing.com
Survey Pro	iMagic Software	www.imagicsurveysoftware.com
Survey Software	SurveyConnect	www.surveyconnect.com

Product	Company	Web Site
Survey Time	Qualtrics Labs	www.surveytime.com
Survey Tools for Windows	William Steinberg Consultants	www.notjustsurveys.com
Survey.com	Survey.com	www.survey.com
SurveyAll	Surveyall.com	www.surveyall.com
SurveyBuilder 2.0	ComCult Research GmbH	www.comcult.de
SurveyCaster	NetCasters	www.surveycaster.com
SurveyConsole	SurveyConsole	www.surveyconsole.com
Surveyetc	Surveyetc	www.surveyetc.com
SurveyEXPERT	Quantum Performance Solutions	www.surveyexpert.com
Surveyforms	Tuglet.com	www.surveyforms.net
SurveyKey	JetMan Productions, Inc.	www.surveykey.com
SurveyLogix	Sparklit Networks	www.surveylogix.com
SurveyMaster	Change Systems	www.surveymaster.com
SurveyMetrix	Sometrix	www.sometrix.com.au
SurveyMonkey	Survey Monkey.com	www.surveymonkey.com
SurveyOne	Surveyone.com	www.surveyone.com
Surveyor	Videlicet	www.videlicet.com
Surveyor Manager	Qualintra	www.qualintra.com
SurveyPro 3.0-with NetCollect Plugin	Apian Software	www.apian.com
SurveyQuest	Sonic Software	www.sqst.com
SurveyReaction.com	Website Reactions, LLC	www.surveyreaction.com
SurveyShare Online Survey Tool	SurveyShare Inc.	www.surveyshare.com
SurveySite Online Market Research	SurveySite	www.surveysite.com

(Continued)

(Continued)

Product	Company	Web Site
SurveySolutions Express	Perseus Development Corporation	http://express.perseus.com
SurveySolutions Pro	Perseus Development Corporation	www.perseus.com
SurveySuite	Intercom	http://intercom.virginia.edu
SurveyTracker	Training Technologies	www.surveytracker.com
SurveyTracker	Pearson Education	www.pearsonncs.com
SurveyView	Research Systems	www.resys.se
SurveyView SQ	Research Systems	www.surveyview.com
SurveyWerks	SurveyWerks	www.surveywerks.com
Surveywriter	SurveyWriter	www.surveywriter.com
SurveyZ	Qualtrics Labs	www.surveyz.com
sysFormer	sysFormer	www.sysformer.de
SySurvey	Syclick	www.sysurvey.com
Tendenci—Web surveys on your Web site	Tendenci Web Marketing Software	www.tendenci.com
Test, Survey & Ballot	GiftTool Inc.	www.gifttool.com
The Survey System	Creative	www.surveysystem.com
TurnFriendly	FIPROX	www.turnfriendly.com
TwoWay Survey	Parnova	www.parnova.com
Ultimate Survey	Prezza Technologies	www.prezzatech.com
Umfrage 2	Hanewald— Software und Webdesign	www.hanewald.info
Umfragecenter/ Survey Center	Globalpark	www.globalpark.de
Umfragen-Software für Online- Umfragen	Scharf-Marketing	www.way2business.de

Product	Company	Web Site
Universal Questionnaire	i-GRasp	www.universalquestionnaire.com
uSurvey	Ubiquity Software Limited	www.usuite.com
VentureFeedback .com	Insync Software	www.venturefeedback.com
VForm	Varitools	www.varitools.com
ViewsFlash	Cogix Corporation	www.cogix.com
Vista	Vanguard Software Corporation	www.vanguardsw.com
VitalStatistix	Soft Corner	www.soft-corner.com
Warp-it	RM PLUS	www.rmplus.si
Web Questionnaire 3.0	CompressWeb	www.compressweb.com
Web Survey Toolbox	Aaron Powers	http://WebSurveyToolbox.org
Web Surveys	QEverything	www.qeverything.com
Web Surveys	Visualnet Media, Inc.	www.visualnetmedia.com
Web Surveys	Rytan and Associates	www.rytan.net/web.html
Web Surveys	The London School of Economics and Political Science	http://websurveys.lse.ac.uk
Web Surveys	Titanic Marketing	www.titanicmarketing.com
Web Surveys	Public Policy Research Lab	www.survey.lsu.edu/services.html
Web Surveys	Regional Educational Technology Center (RETC)	www.retc.fordham.edu
Web Surveys	NetStrategies	www.netstrategies.com
Web Surveys	Bolt	Peters User Experience	www.boltpeters.com
Web-Based Survey	In-Touch	www.intouchsurvey.com

(Continued)

(Continued)

Product	Company	Web Site
webCiter	BESTCite	www.bestcite.com
WebMine	IDEACore	www.ideacore.com
webpolls.de	webpolls.de	www.webpolls.de
WebQA	CustomFAQs Solutions	www.customfaqs.com
WebRespond	Gollmer, S.	http://people.cedarville.edu
WebSurv	AndersonBell Corp	www.andersonbell.com
WebSurvent	CfMC	www.cfmc.com
WebSurveyor	WebSurveyor Corporation	www.websurveyor.com
WinSurvey 2005	AceBIT	www.winsurvey.com
wiredsurvey	Wiredsurvey.com	www.wiredsurvey.com
World Wide Web Survey Assistant	S-Ware	www.mohsho.com
YourThoughts.com Surveys	YourThoughts .com	www.yourthoughts.com
Zacra Interactive	Zarca Interactive	www.zarca.com
ZClasses Survey/ quiz product	Zope.org	www.zope.org
ZipSurvey	Corporate Survey.com	www.zipsurvey.com
Zoomerang	MarketTools	www.zoomerang.com

Survey research codes of ethics can be found at the following:

Name of Organization	Web Site
American Association for Public Opinion Research	www.aapor.org
American Statistical Association, Survey Research Methods Section	www.amstat.org
Council of American Survey Research Organizations	www.casro.org/ codeofstandards.cfm
National Council on Public Polls	www.ncpp.org

Appendix B

Probability Sampling Procedures for Closed Populations

Simple Random Sampling

To select someone "at random" from a given population means that everyone in the population has the same chance of being selected. A "simple random sample" is a sample in which every subset of the population, of a certain sample size, has an equal chance of being selected. The first step in selecting a random sample is to secure (or create) a sampling frame. Sampling frames such as rosters, membership lists, and directories are usually ordered in some way: alphabetically, by department, or by serial number. First, randomize the sampling frame. For example, in Microsoft Excel, this is simply a matter of assigning a random number to each entry on the list using Excel's random number function. Once each element is assigned a random number, the list can be sorted by the random number and a subset of units selected.

Example B.1

To select a simple random sample from a population of 12,000 students at a university, begin with the registrar's list of all students. Randomize the list by assigning each student a random number in the range 00,000 to 12,000. Sort the list by the random numbers. Select the first 200 names, for example, from the list.

Systematic Sampling

A systematic sample is a variation on the simple random sample, in which every *n*th element of a population is selected. As in the simple random sample, this procedure begins with a sampling frame. In this case, however, instead of simply choosing the first 200 names from a randomized list, you would choose every *n*th person on the list. If *n* = 2, then every second person would be selected; if *n* = 3, every third person would be selected; and so on. The distance between each element selected for participation is called the *skip interval*. The first element selected from the list should be selected randomly; this is easily accomplished using Microsoft Excel or some other spreadsheet software on which the list is stored. This procedure ensures that elements from all sectors of the sampling frame are selected.

Example B.2

Suppose you wanted to select a sample of 100 from a list of the 2,000 employees of a company. You would first obtain the list of all employees, identify a random starting row on the list, and then choose every 20th name on the list for the sample.

Stratified Sampling

Selecting a stratified sample is a two-stage procedure. First, divide the population into subgroups (strata); second, select either a simple random sample or a systematic sample for each subgroup. Common stratification variables include gender, age, membership status, and job category. This procedure is useful if there is a chance that a simple random sample will yield disproportionately large numbers of participants in one or more categories. For example, when surveying department managers at a corporation, simple random sampling might, purely by chance, yield a result containing all men and no women: a sample that may not be representative of the population. To correct for this sampling error, the population could be stratified by gender before selecting percentages of respondents that reflect the population percentages.

Example B.3

To select a stratified sample of 400 faculty members from four colleges at a university, you could first stratify the sampling frame by college. Then, using each stratum as a separate sampling frame, select a simple random sample of 100 respondents from within each college.

Cluster Sampling

When the target population is especially large, cluster sampling is a useful approach. A cluster is a preexisting group in a population. Obvious clusters include classes in a school, schools in a district, local chapters of a national organization, and so on. Any of the procedures mentioned above—simple random sampling, systematic sampling, or stratified sampling—may be used to select clusters from a population. Each individual in the selected cluster is invited to participate in the survey.

Cluster sampling also can be used as the first step in a multistage sampling procedure. First, a sample of clusters is drawn from the population; then, individuals from within each cluster are randomly selected.

Example B.4

Say you are interested in surveying nurses employed by a national health care provider. You could begin by obtaining a master list of all member hospitals in the United States and stratify them by region of the country: Northeast, Southeast, Southwest, and Northwest. Then, randomly select five hospitals from each region, and get the lists of all nurses at those hospitals. Finally, draw a simple random sample of nurses from each hospital, and e-mail each one an invitation to participate in the survey.

Appendix C

Basic Demographic Questionnaire

Screen 1 of 2

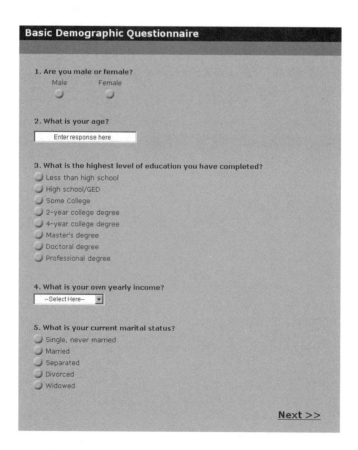

Screen 2 of 2

Basic Demographic Questionnaire

6. What is your religious affiliation?

- ○ Protestant Christian
- ○ Roman Catholic
- ○ Evangelical Christian
- ○ Jewish
- ○ Muslim
- ○ Hindu
- ○ Buddist
- ○ Other (please specify)

> [   ]

7. What is your race/ethnicity?

- ○ White
- ○ African-American
- ○ Hispanic
- ○ Asian
- ○ Pacific Islander
- ○ Native American
- ○ Other (please specify)

> [   ]

8. What is your occupation?

> [Enter response here]

<< Back   Done >>

Appendix D

Sample E-Mail Invitation

Example of E-Mail Invitation

From: Student Life Programs
To: [e-mail address]
Subject: Campus Climate Survey

Dear Student,

You have been randomly selected to participate in a survey about the campus climate at Sun State University. We are interested in your opinions about some of the university's policies, your classes, extracurricular activities, and the accessibility of learning resources. Your participation in this research is very important as it represents the views of many of your classmates.

The survey takes about 10 minutes and is completely voluntary and confidential. Your name will not be linked to your responses in any way. The data will be used to evaluate current university policies and programs.

To participate in the survey, please click on the following link:

www.universitywebsurvey.com

and use this password to identify yourself as an eligible participant: [password].

If you have any questions or need help, please e-mail Susan Staffer at sstaffer@sunstate.edu.

Thank you,
Susan Staffer

P.S. Each survey participant will receive a $10 gift certificate for the campus bookstore. After you complete the survey you will receive instructions on how to claim your gift.

Appendix E

Sample Snail Mail Invitation

Sun State

February 11, 2007

Dear _____,

You are invited to participate in a survey being conducted by Dr. Terry Smith, a faculty member in the Department of Online Studies at Sun State University. Your name was randomly selected from the student body list.

The project is about student experiences with online courses. If you decide to participate, you will be asked to complete a brief online survey. It should take about 10 minutes.

Participation in the project is voluntary and confidential; responses from individual participants will not be published. Data will be pooled and published in aggregate form only. Identifying information, such as your name or e-mail address will be replaced with random identification numbers. Additionally, the information you provide will be kept secure and will not be viewed by anyone but the researcher.

To participate in the survey please go to the following web site:

www.universitywebsurvey.com

Use this password to identify yourself as an eligible participant: [password].

In order to complete this project on time, we would appreciate it if you would go to the web site and complete the questionnaire by [date]. If you have any questions about the research project, you may contact Dr. Smith at: 555-555-5555 or tsmith@sunstate.edu.

Thank you,

Dr. Terry Smith

Professor of Online Studies

P.S. Each survey participant will receive a $10 gift certificate for the campus bookstore. After you complete the survey you will receive instructions on how to claim your gift.

Appendix F

Review of Basic Summary Statistics

Mean

The mean is the arithmetical average of a set of observations and is probably the most commonly used method of describing what is typical in a distribution. The mean is computed by summing the scores and dividing by the number of scores in the set. Here are the ages of 6 students who participated in a class evaluation survey:

22	25	18	20	19	22

The sum of these six values is 126, so the mean is 126/6 = 21.

One problem with the mean is that it is susceptible to the influence of *outliers*. Outliers are scores that lie an extreme distance away from the other scores in a distribution. What constitutes *extreme* is largely up to the data analyst. Some take the view that any data point more than 3 standard deviations away from the mean is an outlier; others apply a more subjective approach, looking at individual questionnaire items and applying different criteria to each one depending on the overall look of the distribution. As an illustration, let's revisit the ages of the 6 students mentioned above and add a seventh student:

22	25	18	20	19	22	65

By adding the seventh student (65 years), the mean of ages becomes 27.28. While the mean is correct, it may not accurately reflect the "typical" situation. The strategies for dealing with outliers when looking at a typical value include the following:

- Ignoring—act as if the outlier isn't there and proceed with analysis as planned (bad solution)
- Deleting—remove the data point from the distribution (worse solution)
- Accommodating—leave the outlier in the data description and provide an explanation (good option)
- Using the median—a better indicator of central tendency because it is not affected by the presence of outliers (best option)

The mean is a logical choice for summarizing interval data such as age, test scores, money, or time. It is common practice to treat responses on attitude scales as interval data;[1] therefore, the mean can be used to summarize a set of attitude scores. Table F1 shows the mean ratings on a teaching evaluation questionnaire that uses a standard "strongly agree" to "strongly disagree" scale.

Table F.1   Mean Ratings on Class Evaluation Survey (1 = Strongly Agree, 4 = Strongly Disagree)

Item	Mean Score
The goals of the course were clear to me.	1.33
The instructor was well prepared for class sessions.	1.25
The course lectures were interesting.	1.86
I enjoyed studying for this class.	2.04
I would recommend this class to other students.	1.56

Median

The median is the middle value in a distribution; half the observations are above the median, and half are below it. To determine the median, first list the values in order from the smallest to largest, then count to the middle. If you have an odd number of values, the median is the number in the middle; if you have an even number of observations, the median is the average of the middle two values. Say, you collected salary data for 6 midlevel managers at a corporation. These are the salaries in thousands of dollars:

114   65   80   78   72   55

First, order the data from the lowest to highest:

55   65   72   78   80   114

Then, find the midpoint; in this case, because there are an even number of data points, we will need to average the two middle values. The median salary is $(72 + 78)/2 = 75$. In practice, you will most likely have more than 6 observations; in this case, the median can easily be located on a frequency distribution as it will be the data point that represents the 50th percentile.

Although the mean is the most popular statistic for summarizing interval data, when the data are skewed by an outlier, as in our previous example, the mean does not provide an accurate picture of the data. In these situations, the median is a better indicator of what is typical because the median is a robust statistic that is not influenced by outliers.

The median is an appropriate summary statistic when reporting the results of ranking questions. For example, say you asked respondents to rank seven problems facing their community by giving a rank of 1 to the most important problem, a rank of 2 to the next most important one, and so on. You could compute the median for each problem that was ranked. Example F.1 presents the ranks that were assigned to the problem of "crime" by 9 respondents. Because the data are already in order, it is easy to see that the median rank is 3.

Example F.1

1, 2, 2, 2, 3, 4, 5, 5, 7

Mode

The mode is the most frequently occurring value in a set of scores. To determine the mode, you might again order the values as shown above and then count the number of times each value appears. In the age data above there were two 22-year-old students; therefore, the mode is 22. There is no mode for the salary data (no value occurred more than once). The frequency distribution of attitude scores in Table F.2 reveals that the mode is 100. The mode is the summary statistic most often used when reporting nominal data such as gender, major in college, music genre, and so on. A data set can have two (bimodal) or more (multimodal) modes.

Range

The range is the difference between the largest and the smallest values in a distribution. It tells us about the spread, or dispersion, in the data. The range is a limited statistic because it depends on only two numbers for its

Table F.2   Distribution of Attitude Scores

Score	No. Obtaining Each Score
100	8
96	7
94	3
93	4
91	3
90	1
22	1
14	1
10	2

value and, like the mean, can be greatly exaggerated by outliers. Recall the example of the ages of 7 students:

22   25   18   20   19   22   65

The range of these values is 65 − 18 = 47; that's a wide range of student ages. Removing the outlier (65) reduces the range to 7 (25 − 18 = 7). The range is often reported so that readers have a context for interpreting other summary statistics such as the mean, median, or mode.

Standard Deviation

Like the range, standard deviation is a measure of variability. Unlike the range, however, standard deviation takes into account all the data points in a distribution. Standard deviation indicates how close to the mean the observations are, on average. If all the observations are the same, the standard deviation is 0. The more spread out the observations are, the larger the standard deviation. Put another way, the larger the standard deviation, the more variation there is in the data. The scores in Example F.2 are from three groups of respondents. Each group has the same mean, but the standard deviations are different.

Example F.2

Means and standard deviations for three groups of scores:

Group A: 15   15   15   15   15   15   15 (mean = 15, *SD* = 0)

Group B: 14   14   14   15   16   16   16 (mean = 15, *SD* = 0.93)

Group C: 0   5   10   15   20   25   30 (mean = 15, *SD* = 10)

As you can see, Group A has no variability ($SD = 0$), and Group C has the most variability ($SD = 10$). The distance of the individual scores from the mean determines the size of the standard deviation. Group C's scores vary greatly from the mean of 15, hence the large standard deviation of 10.

Although it would be easy to compute the standard deviation and the other summary statistics for seven scores by hand, it is unlikely that your survey data will contain only seven values. When you are dealing with hundreds or thousands of data points, it is necessary to let a software program compute these values for you. Every statistical software package is capable of doing this; you will only need to determine the proper commands and, of course, be able to interpret the results.

Note

1. Recall from our earlier discussion that attitude scales are really ordinal because the distance between "very effective" and "effective" is not necessarily equal to the distance between "effective" and "not effective."

Appendix G

Sample of SurveyMonkey's Basic Results Report

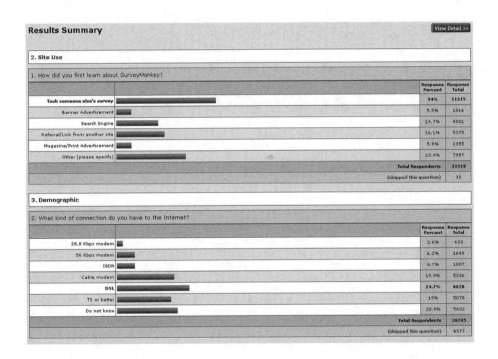

3. Where are you located?

	Response Percent	Response Total
United States	72.5%	18679
Other Country	27.5%	7097
Total Respondents		25776
(skipped this question)		7551

4. Future Directions (continued)

4. Are you satisfied with the overall usability of SurveyMonkey? If not, tell us how we can improve...

	Response Percent	Response Total
Haven't used it yet	65.4%	14952
Yes	31.3%	7151
No	3.4%	771
Total Respondents		22874
(skipped this question)		10458

5. What other features would you like to see added to SurveyMonkey?

Total Respondents		4399
(skipped this question)		28926

5. Future Directions

6. The following features may be added to SurveyMonkey in the near future. Please rate the importance of the following features.

	Very Important	Important	Somewhat Important	Not Important	Response Total
Survey templates	56% (10114)	32% (5794)	9% (1706)	3% (583)	18197
Increased multi-lingual support	22% (3895)	29% (4969)	25% (4277)	24% (4180)	17321
Multiple Users per Account	33% (5762)	35% (6171)	22% (3802)	10% (1699)	17434
Graphical charts of response data	51% (9076)	32% (5754)	11% (1994)	5% (976)	17800
Increased Export Functionality	47% (8181)	34% (5910)	13% (2269)	6% (1113)	17473
Total Respondents					18973
(skipped this question)					14352

Glossary

ALT tag a command that is inserted in a document that specifies how the document, or a portion of the document, should be formatted.

census a set of data collected from every member of a population.

closed-ended question any of a variety of survey questions that include lists of response options.

confidence interval a range within which the true population value of a measurement may lie.

cookie a collection of information, usually including a user name and the current date and time, stored on the local computer of a person using the World Wide Web.

correlation a measure of the strength of the linear relationship between two variables.

double-barreled question a type of question that asks about more than one issue in a single question. This may result in inaccuracies in the attitudes being measured for the question.

download the process of copying a file from an online service to one's own computer.

dropouts survey respondents who begin a questionnaire and abandon it before finishing.

eligibility criteria conditions that permit or exclude certain individuals from participation in a survey.

format to specify the properties, particularly the visible properties, of an object. For example, word processing applications allow you to format text, which involves specifying the font, alignment, margins, and other properties.

hyperlink an element in an electronic document that links to another place in the same document or to an entirely different document.

java applet a small program that can be sent along with a Web page to a user. Applets are used to provide interactive features to Web applications that cannot be provided by HTML.

leading question a type of question that is phrased in a way that suggests to the respondent that the researcher expects a certain answer (i.e., it "leads" the respondent).

margin of error measure of how precise the data are.

mean the arithmetical average, obtained by adding all the values of a measurement and dividing by the total count.

median the middle value of a sequential group of values.

Minitab a computer program designed to perform basic and advanced statistics.

mode the most frequently observed response.

nonrespondents individuals who have been invited to participate in a survey and choose not to respond.

open-ended question a question that does not include a list of response options.

operating system the most important program that runs on a computer. Every general-purpose computer must have an operating system to run other programs. Operating systems perform basic tasks, such as recognizing input from the keyboard, sending output to the display screen, keeping track of files and directories on the disk, and controlling peripheral devices such as disk drives and printers.

outliers scores that lie an extreme distance away from the other scores in a distribution.

pixel short for "picture element," a pixel is a single point in a graphic image.

population   the total group of respondents of interest.

pretest   an examination of the survey by a group of respondents before the survey is deployed to the full sample. It is used to uncover potential problems in the survey instrument or method.

p **value**   the probability of seeing results as extreme as or more extreme than those actually observed if in fact there was no relationship between the variables you're testing.

reliability   the extent to which a measure provides consistent results across repeated testing.

respondent   the survey participant.

response option   a possible answer to a closed-ended question.

sample   a subgroup of selected respondents derived from your target population.

sampling frame   the list of all elements in the population.

SAS   an acronym for Statistical Analysis System, software for the statistical analysis of data.

SPSS   an acronym for Statistical Package for the Social Sciences, software for the statistical analysis of data.

standard deviation a measure of dispersion. It indicates how much values vary around the mean.

target population   the entire group of possible respondents to your survey question. Because it is improbable that you will survey every individual in your target population, you must survey a smaller subgroup of your population, known as a sample.

URL   abbreviation of uniform resource locator, the global address of documents and other resources on the World Wide Web. The first part of the address indicates what protocol to use, and the second part specifies the Internet provider (IP) address or the name of the domain where the resource is located. For example, the two URLs below point to two different files at the domain pcwebopedia .com—the first specifies an executable file that should be fetched using the FTP protocol, and the second specifies a Web page that should be fetched using the HTTP protocol

ftp //www.pcwebopedia.com/stuff.exe

http //www.pcwebopedia.com/index.html

validity   refers to whether the measurement tool (i.e., the survey question) accurately and appropriately measures the concept under consideration.

Web survey   a type of survey methodology used to deliver data results of the survey. Advantages include rapid response rate, very low cost, and increased respondent flexibility.

wizard   part of a computer program that guides users through steps in a process—for example, writing letters, creating PowerPoint shows, or importing data from one software program into another.

References

Able Access Net. (1999). Retrieved October 24, 2005, from www.jmk.su.se/globa199/access/dyslexia/statdys.html

Academic Computing and Communications Center. (n.d.). Designing accessible Web pages. Retrieved November 3, 2005, from www.uic.edu.depts/accc/webpub/webaccess.html

Alreck, P. L., & Settle, R. B. (1995). *The survey research handbook* (2nd ed.). Chicago: Irwin.

Babbie, E. (2004). *The practice of social research* (10th ed.). Belmont, CA: Wadsworth/Thompson Learning.

Bachmann, D., Elfrink, & Vazzana, G. (1996). Tracking the progress of e-mail vs. snail mail. *Marketing Research, 8* (2), 30–35.

Bauman, S., Jobity, N., Airey, J., & Atak, H. (2000, May 20). Invites, intros and incentives: Lessons from a Web survey. Paper presented at the American Association for Public Opinion Research Annual Conference, Portland, OR.

Bernard, M., Liao, C., & Mills, M. (2001). Determining the best online font for older adults. *Usability News*. Retrieved November 14, 2005, from http://psychology.wichita.edu/surl/usabilitynews/3W/fontSR.htm

Bernard, M., & Mills, M. (2000). So, what size and type font should I use on my Website? *Usability News*. Retrieved November 14, 2005, from http://psychology.wichita.edu/surl/usabilitynews/2S/font.htm

Bernard, M., Mills, M., Peterson, M., & Storrer, K. (2001). A comparison of popular online fonts: Which is best and when? *Usability News*. Retrieved November 14, 2005, from http://psychology.wichita.edu/surl/usabilitynews/3S/font.htm

Couper, M. P. (2000). Web surveys: A review of issues and approaches. *Public Opinion Quarterly, 64,* 464–494.

Couper, M. P., Balir, J., & Triplett, T. (1999). A comparison of mail and e-mail for a survey of employees in federal statistical agencies [Electronic version]. *Journal of Official Statistics, 15,* 39–56.

Couper, M. P., Traugott, M., & Lamias, M. (2001). Web survey design and administration. *Public Opinion Quarterly, 65,* 230–253.

Dillman, D. A. (1978). *Mail and telephone surveys: The total design method.* New York: Wiley.

Dillman, D. A. (2000). *Mail and Internet surveys: The tailored design method* (2nd ed.). New York: Wiley.

Dillman, D. A., & Bowker, D. K. (2001). The Web questionnaire challenge to survey methodologists. Retrieved September 15, 2005, from www.sesrc.wsu.edu/dillman/papers.htm

Dillman, D. A., Smyth, J. D., Christian, L. M., & Stern, M. J. (2002). Multiple answer questions in self-administered surveys: The use of check-all-that-apply and forced-choice question formats. Retrieved October 12, 2006, from www.sesrc.wsu.edu/dillman/papers.htm

Dillman, D., Tortora, R. D., & Bowker, D. (1998). Principles for constructing web surveys. Retrieved December 8, 2005, from http://survey.sesrc.wsu.edu/dillman/papers.htm

Dillman, D. A., Tortora, R. D., Conrad, J., & Bowker, D. (1998). Influence on plain vs. fancy design on response rates of Web surveys. Retrieved December 2, 2005, from http://survey.sesrc.wsu.edu/dillman/papers.htm

Evangelista, F., Albaum, G., & Poon, P. (1999). An empirical test of alternative theories of survey response behavior. *Journal of the Market Research Society, 41*(2), 227–244.

Fink, A. (2003). *How to manage, analyze, and interpret survey data* (2nd ed.). Thousand Oaks, CA: Sage.

Fowler, F. J. (2002). *Survey research methods* (3rd ed.). Thousand Oaks, CA: Sage.

Göritz, A. (2004). The impact of material incentives on response quantity, response quality, sample composition, survey outcome, and cost in online access panels. *International Journal of Market Research, 46*(3), 327–345.

Göritz, A. (2005). Incentives in Web-based studies: What to consider and how to decide. Retrieved November 29, 2005, from www.websm.org

Gouveia-Pisano, J. A. (n.d.). Tips for preparing and delivering presentations. Retrieved January 1, 2006, from www.aphanet.org/AM/Template.cfm?Section=Search&section=Advanced_Training_Credentialing&template=/CM/ContentDisplay.cfm&ContentFileID=1210

Granello, D. H., & Wheaton, J. E. (2004). Using Web-based surveys to conduct counseling research. In J. W. Bloom & G. R. Walz (Eds.) *Cybercounseling and cyberlearning: An encore* (pp. 287–306). Alexandria, VA: American Counseling Association.

Groves, R. M. (1989). *Survey errors and survey costs.* Wiley-Interscience: Haboken.

Hamilton, M. B. (2004). Online survey response rates and times. Retrieved July 3, 2005, from www.supersurvey.com

Hill, R. (1998). What sample size is "enough" in Internet survey research? *Interpersonal Computing and Technology: An Electronic Journal for the 21st Century, 6*(3–4). Retrieved October 17, 2006, from www.emoderators.com/ipct-j/1998/n3-4/hill.html

Kish, L. (1995). *Survey sampling.* New York: Wiley.

Kittleson, M. (1997). Determining effective follow-up of e-mail surveys. *American Journal of Health Behavior, 21*(3), 193–196.

Kwak, N., & Radler, B. (2002). A comparison between mail and Web surveys: Response pattern, respondent profile, and data quality. *Journal of Official Statistics, 18*(2), 257–273.

Levy, P., & Lemeshow, S. (1999). *Sampling of populations: Methods and applications* (3rd ed.). Wiley Series in Survey Methodology. New York: Wiley-Interscience.

Los Alamos National Laboratory. (2001). Preparing a poster exhibit. Retrieved December 28, 2005, from http://set.lanl.gov/programs/cif/Resource/Presentation/PosterS.htm

Martin, P., & Bateson, P. (1986). *Measuring behavior: An introductory guide.* Cambridge, UK: Cambridge University Press.

McCullough, D. (1998). Web-based market research, the dawning of a new era. *Direct Marketing, 61*(8), 36–39.

Morrison, S., & Noyes, J. (2003). A comparison of two computer fonts: Serif versus ornate san serif. *Usability News.* Retrieved November 14, 2005, from http://psychology.wichita.edu/surl/usabilitynews/52/UK_font.htm

Newman, C. (2000). Considering the colorblind. Retrieved October 25, 2005, from http://webtechniques.com/archives/2000/08

Paolo, A. M., Bonaminio, G. A., Gibson, C., Partidge, T., & Kallail, K. (2000). Response rate comparisons of e-mail and mail-distributed student evaluations. *Teaching and Learning in Medicine, 12*(2), 81–84.

Pearson, J., & Levine, R. A. (2003). Salutations and response rates to online surveys. Retrieved May 2, 2005, from www.stanford.edu/~jpearson/salutations.pdf

Pew Global Attitudes. (2006, February 21). *Truly a World Wide Web: Globe going digital* (Project Report). Washington, DC: Author.

Reja, U., Lozar Manfreda, K., Hlebec, V., & Vehovar, V. (2003). Open-ended vs. closed-ended questions in Web questionnaires. Advances in methodology and statistics. *Metodoloski zvezki, 19,* 159–177.

Schaefer, R., & Dillman, D. A. (1998). Development of a standard e-mail methodology: Results of an experiment. *Public Opinion Quarterly, 62*(3), 378–397.

Scheaffer, L. R., Mendenhall, W., & Ott, R. L. (2006). *Elementary survey sampling* (6th ed.). Belmont, CA: Duxbury Press.

Smyth, J. D., Dillman, D. A., Christian, L. M., & Stern, M. J. (2006). Comparing check-all and forced-choice question formats in Web surveys. *Public Opinion Quarterly, 70,* 66–77.

Truell, A., & Goss, P. (2002). Business education leaders compare e-mail and regular mail survey research. *Journal of Technology Studies, 18*(1), 81–83.

Van den Broeck, J., Argeseanu Cunningham, S., Eeckels, R., & Herbst, K. (2005). Data cleaning: Detecting, diagnosing, and editing data abnormalities. *PLoS Med, 2*(10), e267.

Walsh, J. P., Kiesler, S., Sproul, L. S., & Hesses, B. W. (1992). Self-selected and randomly selected respondents in a computer network survey. *Public Opinion Quarterly, 56,* 241–244.

Wolfram Research. (n.d.). Mathworld. Retrieved December 7, 2005, from http://mathworld.wolfram.com/Box-and-WhiskerPlot.html

Index

About the Authors

Valerie M. Sue is an associate professor and director of the graduate program in the Department of Communication at California State University, East Bay. She teaches courses in research methods, survey research methods, statistics, and communication theory. Her research interests include citizens' use of mass media for political information and survey methodology. She has designed and participated in numerous survey projects and is a regular research consultant to a variety of academic and professional clients. She is a graduate of Stanford University, where she earned a PhD in communication.

Lois A. Ritter is an assistant professor in the Nursing and Health Science Department at California State University, East Bay. She teaches courses in community health and evaluation. She also is a research manager at Walter R. McDonald & Associates, Inc. She has worked in health care and education for over 20 years and has extensive experience in conducting needs assessments and evaluation. She earned an EdD, with an emphasis on learning and instruction, from the University of San Francisco and an MS from San Francisco State University. She is continuing her studies at California State University, East Bay, to earn an MA in anthropology with a minor in statistics.